How to Change a Flat on a Unicycle:

Volume II of
The Travels of
Senator & Wendy V

- © 2007 by Wendy V. All rights reserved. No part of this publication may be reproduced or transmitted in any form or by any means, electronic or mechanical, including photocopy, recording, or any information storage and retrieval system, without the prior written consent of the author and/or publisher.

- cover photography © 2007 by Spencer Levy.

ISBN: 978-0-99150-931-7

for Senator—

...ah made dis for yew...

"I know very well, how little reputation is to be got by writings which require neither genius nor learning, nor indeed any other talent, except a good memory, or an exact *journal*….. And, it is highly probable, that such travelers who shall hereafter visit the countries described in this work of mine, may by detecting my errors, (if there be any) and adding many new discoveries of their own, jostle me out of vogue, and stand in my place, making the world forget that ever I was an author."

Dr. Lemuel Gulliver,
Gulliver's Travels

Table of Contents

Introduction	i.
Three Dog Night	1
Thousands of Miles, Hundreds of Feet and Dozens of Degrees	19
Czech, Please	41
May I Use One of Your 43 Bathrooms?	53
The Paperback Writer Gets a Ticket to Ride	81
Then Maybe One Day	97
Afterword	121
Appendix	123

Author's Note #1

See Author's Note, *How to Read a Compass in the Dark.*

Author's Note #2

They say a picture is worth 1,000 words. As I have never had any particular luck with cameras-- three duds to date--, I have tried to present a written photo album instead. By the mathematical equation, this edition presently contains about forty pictures. Perhaps one day you can all come over and eat popcorn in the dark, while we project slides of the text onto a blank wall, narrating every word in cadence with your snores.

~Wendy V
June 2007

Introduction

Congratulations! You made it to Volume II, which means one of three things: 1. you enjoyed Volume I enough to continue the madness, 2. you are a friend/relative who will feel guilty if you don't read Wendy's newest book (*why couldn't she just color a picture for our refrigerator?*), or 3. you mistakenly received this copy due to a routine United States Postal Service shipping error and are just curious enough about a book with a glittering piano and feather boa the cover, written by an author without a real last name. Whatever the case, the pages in your hands chronicle another two years of our travels.

At some point, we decided to take on the challenge of visiting all fifty states. By the end of Volume I, we had tackled twenty-three of them. If you were counting states in the first book, first of all, you have too much time on your hands. Secondly, you probably came up short since we took a brief camping trip to Michigan, which I failed to report upon. To make sure you got your money's worth, here is the omitted synopsis: fighting traffic to get up the west coast of Michigan, hiking to a lighthouse, being attacked by man-and-woman-eating flies on the beach, biking, making calzones over an open fire, rain, reading Hawthorne by lantern, rain, wandering, rain, debating, rain, and packing it up early for a dry bed and pizza at home. But I digress...

Though we still planned and executed several trips, we traveled a little less during the period covered in this book. This was partly due to various projects and expenses on the home front, and partly due to the fact that we managed to evade any wedding invitations for quite some time. The tradition of things not going according to plan, however, was kept alive and well. As you may remember, this was firmly established during the first two years with such events as a plane change, a multi-state power outage, an uninvited rodent roommate, touring the Great Plains instead of Great Britain, and an unexpected death in the family. The next two years would demand almost as much flexibility on our part.

~Wendy V
June 2007

Chapter 1
Three Dog Night: Mid-October 2005

Life, in general, tends to be full of inconvenient surprises. You might be invited to two equally appealing events on the same day at the same time. You also might be walking along the sidewalk on your way to an important interview for a scholarship and trip and skin your knee for the first time since you were seven. Furthermore, you might empty the contents of your car trunk, check to make sure the keys are in your hand, and then, in a split second, sneeze and drop the keys, which, regretfully, fall through the slit opening just before the trunk door slams shut. Or maybe *you* would not, but I would, and I have. It should come as no surprise then, that when I set out to plan a trip, the unexpected or inconvenient is bound to occur. I just did not expect it to take place on such an enormous scale.

As I have stated, I have a sort of mental list of cities in which I would like to spend extended weekends. Among these are San Diego, Boston, Memphis, and, of course, New Orleans. The Big Easy was a place that I had always dreamed of going. I wanted to experience the jazz, the zydeco, the French/Cajun culture, and heck, maybe even Richard Simmons. I planned to saunter down Bourbon Street in the 150% humidity, smell the sights, and taste the odors.

What I could do without, however, was Mardi Gras. While the crowds, parades, party, and danger appeal to some, I would rather visit in a less popular setting. Besides, I could think of easier ways to obtain plastic beads. Thus, we would meander our way down the Mississippi to the bluesy delta in the autumn.

Roughly seven weeks before we were to leave, my mom called me to give me the update on the world. For various reasons, we have chosen to live our lives t.v.-free. This is not, as some have inquired, for religious or eccentric reasons, but simply because we have better things to do with our time, and it makes us antsy to sit through most shows and their idiotic commercials. While we are still exposed to radio, the internet, and interpersonal communication, my mother has taken it upon herself to be my domestic news correspondent.

This particular evening she called to notify me about a hurricane in southern Louisiana, New Orleans to be exact. She told me how bad it was, doing her best to paint a picture of the flood waters and devastation over the phone. At the time, I did not think much of it. *Okay, thanks. I think we're safe.* She expressed concern about our upcoming trip, and the safety/sanitation issues associated with it. Admittedly, I passed it off as her 'being a mom'. Worrying about stuff like this is in a mom's job description. They take an oath or something.

A day and a half later, when Hurricane Katrina was the only topic of anyone's conversation, it occurred to me that I should probably look into this little thunderstorm. As we surfed the news photos on the internet, I was speechless. Large portions of entire cities were now annexed by the Gulf of Mexico. Starving families and invalids trapped on rooftops awaited rescue while overcrowded shelters spawned the spread of crime and disease.

Often Midwesterners, myself included, can be a cold people when it comes to sympathy for hurricane victims. We jealously point fingers, scolding that they have several days' warning to leave town, whereas our tornadoes can strike in a matter of seconds. While there certainly is a sector of the population that has only themselves to blame for being ravaged by a hurricane, many people never have the viable option of evacuating, due to financial, medical, or logistical dilemmas. I had not been so struck by visual images of human suffering since the terrorist attacks in 2001. It soon became apparent that this was not just a mess that the city or state would quickly sweep up. The next day I canceled our reservations. That is, I tried to. The hotel where we were going to stay no longer had phone service.

Now what? Ah, the eternal question... When our friend Michelle from New York learned of our forced changed in plans, she asked, (after expressing proper sentiment for the hurricane victims), what we were going to do instead. Not known for her subtlety when inviting/begging her friends to come see her, she suddenly had a "great idea". What if we used our vacation time to come back to New York instead? *Gee, I don't know. There were already three chapters about New York in the last book.*

Sure, why not? The only problem was that getting a hotel room in Lower Manhattan on a weekend without three years' notice and six references is next to impossible. No problem; she insisted we stay with her and her husband, Spencer. We were a bit apprehensive, as this would be our first time staying with friends, but we were sufficiently confident that we could all manage to get along together while still staying out of each other's hair for five days, so we booked our familiar flight to La Guardia.

Late Wednesday night, (or early Thursday, if you are one of those *morning* people,) we left our home for Midway Airport. We plodded through the necessary lines, bleary-eyed. It was an easy flight to New York, partially spent contemplating my amazing knack for planning trips just as something major goes haywire. Given my record, we were lucky Mt. St. Helens did not erupt when we went to Washington five months earlier.

Nevertheless, we arrived at Spencer and Michelle's building, and dutifully reported to the lobby attendant. Our friends were still at work, so the attendant would give us their key to let ourselves in. With just enough of a smile to give away his true friendly nature, but enough of a stern façade to remind us that he was on the clock, he quickly nodded a "You're welcome." If we ever get a lobby attendant for our house, I want one like him.

As we approached the door to the apartment, the familiar barks greeted us. December and Vilka did their best impression of guard dogs. This always sounds impressive and possibly even threatening, until we pat their heads and they give up their fierce charade. We repeat this ceremony every time we see them.

"Bark! Bark! Bark! Bark! Oh, it's you guys again. How was your flight? Our humans should be home in a few hours. Make yourselves comfortable. Care for a drink? You will have to excuse our lack of opposable thumbs. We can't reach the counter or open the fridge, but help yourselves to whatever."

After a suitable nap sprawled on the couch, we regrouped and planned the afternoon. We had time to kill until our friends returned from work. The month had already turned chilly, and it looked drizzly out, so we decided, naturally, to take a long walk. We hopped the elevator down to the lobby and bid a friendly adieu to our pal behind the desk. Half-hospitable, half-suspicious, he returned our sentiment with the officious nod. We exited and marched the block over to Broadway Street.

Our first stop was J&R, a large emporium that has expanded into a row of stores offering everything from used cds to refrigerators (unused). We rendered our backpack for inspection by the bouncer at the front door. Darn. We wouldn't be able to swipe any home theatres today. Oblivious people milled about, flipping through the bins of music. I shopped, but far more casually than most. There was just too much to sort through. Once you started, where would you stop?

Furthermore, what is the proper social etiquette when shopping for music around other customers? Unlike your regular retail outlet, when you look at cds, you typically begin at one end and run your jittery fingers down each row until you reach the end of the line, pausing only for interesting pieces, or to try to remember how many copies of *Dark Side of the Moon* you already own. The dilemma: how do you 'pass' someone on this digital highway? Do you taper your speed and remain a row behind him/her, politely distancing your following, or do you cross behind him/her and double back to inspect the missed row later? Then one has to address another fragile issue: what about the rejected candidates from the person you are following? If he/she pulls a cd, reviews it, and places it on top of the stacks, is it fair game for you to grab? Perhaps the establishment of these protocols is a commission for my Essential Other, Senator.

We made a small purchase and left J&R under the furrowed brow of the security guard. Between the cool, rainy weather, and the fact that we had not eaten all day, we were ready to find some New York grub. Actually, I am not sure there is such a thing as 'New York cuisine'. Instead, there is a variety of ethnic foods, most of them deliciously authentic, which accurately reflect the variety of people. Later that evening we were going to be treated to fondue by Spencer and Michelle, so we tried to keep it light.

Nothing grabbed our attention until we were a few doors down from our temporary dwelling. Approaching a small, two-story deli, our noses led us to an Indian cafeteria. The food was sensational, the prices reasonable, the portions sufficient, and the joint crowded. After the patient staff endured our questions and interpreted the names of some of the dishes, we made our selections and climbed the stairs to the seating area. Satisfied with our new secret find and warmed up, we went back to Michelle's and began the reintroductions with their dogs.

After some relaxing reading on a rainy day, we welcomed our friends into their own home. As we visited and they performed their after-work routines, the phone rang. The answering machine picked up immediately, reciting its tired instructions. At such moments there is always that suspenseful pause, when anyone who is not a member of the household feels a little awkward, like he should cover his ears, in case the message contains private information. Not so this time. "Stormtracker, here, kids! The hurricane is moving northeast and will hit Florida on Saturday, Sunday at the latest."

Michelle's mom would provide these periodic updates throughout the weekend. *What is it with these weather-moms?* I was not sure how this affected us in New York, until Michelle explained that she had a relative in Florida. Well in that case, we should follow the progress. After all, we missed the boat completely on Katrina. They turned on the Weather Channel, and I did a very modified and stifled (for the sake of our kind hosts) version of The Weather Channel Dance[*]. We watched plenty of mindless coverage, ("Yeah, this looks like it's gonna' be a wet one. It's either gonna' hit here, or two inches away on this other part of the map. Make sure you have plenty of supplies, especially batteries to be able to catch useful weather reports like this..."). We turned it off and adjourned to the dining room.

Spencer briefed us on the evening's menu, explaining the difference between fondue and *fun*due. We would be

---

[*]See *How to Read a Compass in the Dark.*

experiencing the latter. Within moments, the sterno pot was lit, the cheese and white wine concoction was oozed into the fondue pot, and the plate of steaming vegetables was placed on the table. Okay, show us how it's done.

Senator got the hang of it right away. Take spear in hand. Address prey (vegetables). Go in for the kill. Bring trophy into melted cheese to complete sacrifice. Enjoy. I, on the other hand, was lucky to be able to effectively stab my dinner without it slipping out from under my grip on the plate. Once I mastered the attack, I couldn't get my act together for the essential dip. More vegetables escaped into that cheese pond... The ones that did successfully complete the journey to my mouth were delicious. For someone as uncoordinated as me, however, it could be a great diet gimmick, not unlike eating with chopsticks. I could picture my next book, *Fondues and Fondon'ts: Drop Your Food and Drop the Weight*.

The next morning our roommates were off to work again, and we were off to play again. The second cold, rainy day in New York demanded an initial coffee layer. Michelle told us about Klatch, a tiny coffee shop just behind their building. It sounded like a great place to begin another day on foot. We walked into the narrow shop, down the aisle to the cash register, between two crammed rows of tables. The fare was typical, and so was the clientele, with the exception of Mom-Who-Thinks-She-Is-Exposing-Her-Child-To-Culture-By-Bringing-Him-Somewhere-He-Has-No-Business. The pre-schooler squealed and squeezed himself between the patrons and dangerously close to our coffee and my attitude. As he tore through the napkins and stirrers, his mom kept uttering that disturbingly fake laugh that was supposed to convince us that her monster was adorable, and probably gifted as well. I glared, grabbed my coat, and we took our joe on the road.

We soon traded the screaming attention hound for the serenity and beauty of Trinity Church. As in other trips to New

York, the Eighteenth Century English church and its accompanying graveyard again awed me. The rain splashed across the headstones and cooled off my coffee. Family meeting time: we could either take the subway to Greenwich, or just walk, as originally intended. Due to the destination, we decided to walk.

The destination, as you may have guessed, was our favorite in Greenwich Village: Murray's Cheese Shop. We began the forty-five minute pre-calorie burning walk north, opting to first stop at Bleecker Street Records, just a few doors before Murray's. We walked along several shops, apartment buildings, and groups of leisurely hanger-outers. The store signs changed languages a few times as we traversed various ethnic neighborhoods, finally settling on the familiar Italian.

Prolonging the inevitable fromaggio feast, we stopped at the record store. Ducking inside, we began the flipping ritual. I do not recall finding any treasures on this particular trip, but the selection of music and movies is impressive, given the independent status of the small store. If you ever find that you need a Jimi Hendrix concert poster, an obscure gospel record, a *Texas Chainsaw Massacre* dvd, and a rare Cure cd, this is definitely your place for one-stop shopping.

Normally, we leave BSR, turn right, pause to look in the window of a very artistic bakery, and then continue a few doors down to Murray's. This time, however, a blazing new red and yellow sign greeted us from across the street, as soon as we stepped out of the store. I did not realize that Murray's had grown up since our last trip to New York. The tiny, crowded, old deli counter had morphed into a new sizable, professionally lit and decorated, crowed shop. *How about that? Apparently so people read my first book that business picked up beyond all expectation, forcing them to relocate.* Though some of the romance is always lost when your favorite little 'spot' mainstreams itself, we chose to sell out and go inside after the cheese.

"Hello, welcome to Murray's. Have you been here before?" *Well, actually, not here, but... What's this?! Who is this kid approaching us like a department store floorwalker? What happened to the Old World cheese chopper behind the counter, and his family of efficient cheese weighers and ringer-uppers?* "Over there is our cheese counter. You can take a number and shop around until we call for your order. There's wine in the rear, breads to the left..." *Take a what?* I didn't hear anything else he said. I suppose one could make the argument that a number system worked better than a mob of people edging themselves to the front of the counter to humbly approach the Granter of Cheese, but it sure wasn't nearly as fun. We took our anonymous number and followed the track lighting beams to the flatbread display, ignoring the pyramid of gourmet chocolates. In all fairness, the product quality is as excellent as ever, and Murray's deserves the success, but I was still a bit nostalgic for the aromatically stinky shop across the street, and for the green park bench in front, where we first slathered our pesto on our mozzarella.

Leaving Murray's, we decided to take a slightly different route back to Spencer and Michelle's home. Walking east out of Greenwich, the scenery turned to a dreary landscape of identical apartment buildings. Occasionally a tiny green courtyard was sandwiched between two of them, but for the most part, the view was uninterrupted and uninteresting-- until it started to rain. Now everything took on new life. Residents scampered to close windows and pedestrians darted across slick walkways. As for us, well, once you're wet, you're wet. We still had a good ten blocks to walk, so there was no point in trying to run and dodge the drops.

Finally, we saw the outline of their building. Moments later we were wringing ourselves out as well as we could before entering the sanctuary of the lobby. For some strange reason I felt like I should apologize to the attendant, as though no one else ever comes home dripping across his marble entryway. I wouldn't say he approved, but we got the half-smile from him. We sloshed our way into the elevator and pushed '4'. The doors opened after our very brief ascent and we stepped up to their apartment door. We fumbled with the trusted-houseguests key, and entered the living room.

There was instantly an odor. Nothing was on fire, no old food was left out, and it certainly was not the greeting of potpourri. *Could we be that rank after our long walk in the rain?* I did the subtle turn-and-sniff pit check. It did not seem to be either of us. "Hey!" Senator exclaimed, "There's a third dog here!" We were tired the day before when we arrived, but I think we would have noticed three dogs instead of two. The large, ancient, fluffy beast sidled his way over to welcome us. Meanwhile December and Vilka tried to explain:

> "Well, you see, last night, bark bark bark bark. So our humans said bark bark bark bark. Anyway, this is Farnsworth. He's visiting. And again, help yourself to a beverage."

Our hosts would not be home until late that night, and they had failed to mention Farnsworth's visit, but we were anticipating a good story later.

We changed clothes and flipped through the local entertainment magazines to find something to do that night. Grazing the small print, we saw a free outdoor concert celebration of the Canal Park Restoration. We might not have thought twice about it, had not we seen Lou Reed's name listed as the headliner. The cynical New York songwriter/rocker has built a multi-decade reputation on his poetic lyrics and dreary, punkish song/speak delivery. Also on the bill was Laurie Anderson, accomplished violinist, poet, and performance artist. Senator informed me that the two were dating at the time.

Sure, that sounded like a good time. This time we packed our umbrellas along with a few munchies. Fingering our well-worn street map, we crossed Broadway toward Church Street. Since our route would take us through the World Trade Center plaza, we decided to cut through the enormous lobby of one of the buildings. Odd as it may seem, in large cities, it is sometimes quicker to go *through* a building than to go around it. This, however, was not true in this case. We paused in the beautiful foyer to read some historical and memorial plaques, then looked up to find two roads diverging in a yellow fog. We chose the one to the right, and it did not make all of the difference. This corridor led to an outside covered hallway, which offered lovely views of the city, but not much hope of finding our way out. A few more twists and turns and we were dumped back outside on a very dark sidewalk. At least we were still on the correct side of Manhattan.

It appeared we had come out at a delivery entrance or international smuggling entrance, and we now had two options. *Why were there always choices?* We could continue on our dimly lit path, or risk our lives by crossing six lanes of unforgiving traffic. We continued our shady trailblazing until the New York City Planning Commission came to our rescue. Years ago, some thoughtful engineer had installed a pedestrian crosswalk over the speeding traffic. *Boy I would have felt stupid if we got killed running across traffic only to find a footbridge two blocks down.* We easily made our way across the bridge and toward the Canal Park area, somewhere near Chelsea.

At some point during our travels, the title of Directional Queen was thrust upon me, despite my protests. Senator managed to find his way around just fine for a few decades before meeting me, but he insists that I am some kind of flesh-and-blood compass. If the boy only knew... I began to get a little nervous when I saw no sign of any concerts or events. *It should be very close by.* I was just about to give up and ask a cop for help when we approached an indistinct intersection. To the right, one block was barricaded off, and a few hundred chairs were set up on the street in front of a makeshift trailer stage.

People casually filtered in, coffee in hand, musing about their weather predictions, small town style. Eventually the emcee came on to thank everyone for coming and to announce the celebration of Canal Park's restoration. I think we were the only people in the crowd who could barely locate Canal Park, let alone recall its glory days, demise, and reinstatement. Thankfully, the opening slide show filled us in on enough of the history to allow us to fake it like natives.

A few neighborhood acts performed, and a few poets spouted their devotion to the artistic 'hood. The lowlight of the program was a singing theatre troupe that was supposed to be some ridiculous interpretation of a gypsy band. Instead, the prancing and obnoxious singing of their over-makeuped women and over-festive men made us wonder if we had read the magazine correctly regarding the night's entertainment.

Things took a turn for the better when Laurie Anderson took the stage, though. With grace, elegance, and a soft voice, she performed songs and spoken word poetry, while playing her electric violin beautifully. One of her poems had something to do with spending time alone with her dog romping through the meadows or something or other, but it was surprisingly good. *Perhaps I should write odes to my late pet rats.*

Finally, Lou Reed was introduced. All right. Here we go. Bring it on. He took the stage with only his guitar, looking a bit bedraggled. He performed a few songs, somewhat listlessly, and thanked and goodnighted everyone. We could not tell if he was ill or just bored. Senator imagined the conversation of months before.

"Lou, honey, I've got this Canal Park benefit thing…"
"No way, Laurie."

"But Lou, this is *our* neighborhood."

"No way, Laurie."

"You know how much it would mean to the people-- *our* people. It's no big deal, just a few quick songs, no band or anything."

"No way, Laurie."

"Just as a favor to me?"

"But I'm Lou Reed."

"I know, Sweetie, but please? I'll make it up to you—I promise."

"*(grumbles, growls, mutters)* What am I supposed to wear to this thing?"

Thus, we enjoyed our free concert, and the rain even held off for the most part. We returned to meet our friends at home. Trading stories about our days, we learned that our latest roommate, Farnsworth, was the mostly deaf, sixteen year old dog of Spencer's parents, who were on Long Island for the weekend. For various reasons, Farnsworth would be bunking with all of us for a night or two. We were also usefully informed that if we wanted to get his attention, we would have to speak four octaves below normal, as he could only receive very low-end sounds. This, naturally, ensued in a riotous match of who could call the dog in the deepest voice. Faaaaaaaaahhhhhnsworth! Needless to say, I lost.

Saturday ushered in the return of the drizzle, making for a lazy morning. Spencer had graciously volunteered to prepare brunch for us, which he informed us "is the best meal of the day". When we got up enough ambition to come to the table, we were treated to a fiesta of eggs, beans, and sautéed vegetables in warm tortillas, along with fried potatoes. Yum, yum, and yum.

After lying around visiting and stormtracking, we picked up the same entertainment magazine from the day before. It alerted us to the fact that John Zorn would be performing later that evening in a small venue in the East Village. Mr. Zorn, a rather austere jazz musician, is always experimental and never predictable, which can be a gamble, but is usually rewarding. Our friend Tony, who was living across the drink in New Jersey-- not that there's anything wrong with that-- would join us for the venture.

When Tony arrived, we grabbed our trusty umbrellas and map, and cabbed to the alleged location of The Stone. This time I was sure of our course, but the place was nowhere to be found. We walked back a block, then up two blocks, then over a block, and then decided we were hungry, temporarily giving up. We ducked into a Mexican restaurant, allured by the smells and the lack of rain inside. In simple terms, we tried to explain our destination to our server, and she, in broken English, directed us to a doorway that we had already passed twelve times. We thanked her for a delicious meal and headed back to the intersection. Lo and behold, in three inch stick-on letters of plain black font-- the kind that cost a buck at the hardware store-- on a very plain doorway with no other signs, was The Stone.

During our journey, we theorized that perhaps Mr. Zorn wanted to weed out the average scum like us who might foolishly expect to look up and see his name on the well-lit sign of a music venue. Perhaps we were not worthy. The Great and Powerful Zorn has spoken! We went inside anyway, to a small but packed room with a stage full of various instruments from bass violins to bongos. The performance itself was tight, melodious, and exciting. The only problem was that it was being viewed by us three overtired and goofy kids who could barely contain our muffled giggles as we tried to shake the image of John Zorn as the Wizard of Oz, hiding behind a thick veil and controlling the other musicians with great clouds of smoke enveloping the scene. It was almost as hard as trying not to laugh in church, which, on a few occasions, has also been quite a challenge for me.

The Wizard of Zorn was a tough act to follow, but it was early, so we decided to take in a movie, or, more aptly, go out to one.* We collectively chose *Capote*, partly because we had not heard of most of the other titles. This turned out to be two hours of an accurately fairy-voiced Truman Capote befriending a condemned murderer. I had naively thought the movie would be a more general, biographical approach to his life and writing. Yawn, yawn, and yawn. We broke up the night to go home, get into dry clothes, and reconvene in the morning.

Sunday morning lived up to its name. I twitched and stepped to the Weather Channel jazz, which promised us a lovely, clear autumn day. Perfect. We would walk around the neighborhood during the day, and I could twitch some more later that evening when we took in another concert.

We picked up Jersey Tony (no Mafioso relation), and our hungry quintet walked to a Mexican cantina for the all-imperative brunch. To say we were giddy does not begin to describe our state. I wish I could give you a good reason why. Maybe it was the sun's rare appearance in that week. Maybe it was the vacation vibe, or maybe it was our post-Zorn enlightenment. At any rate, we finally got our orders out, after fits of laughter between introducing each of ourselves to our poor server, and commenting on half of the menu. If he knew what the next hour would hold, he would have cut us off from caffeine right from the start.

---

*This is more significant than it sounds. Our friends are constantly astounded by the fact that, to date, Senator and I have never been out to a movie alone together, generally preferring to view films from the comfort of our home, where our feet don't usually stick to the floor. Indeed, we had only been out to one other movie prior to this. We attended the Metallica rockumentary, *Some Kind of Monster* (highly unrecommended) with five other people. Maybe one day, when the relationship gets really serious, we'll go on a movie date.

It didn't stop there. The table next to us was celebrating a family event, which we invited ourselves to participate in as well. "Hey, how's it going over there? Try the huevos rancheros!" When our meals finally arrived, a few of us ended up with each other's dishes. What should have been a simple and quiet trade ended up in a free-for-all game of musical plates. Here, I offer two items in our defense: 1.)we left a good tip, and 2.)we were entertaining enough that the kitchen sent out complimentary muffins… COMPLI-MENTARY MUFFINS! Even so, if you happened to have been one of the other patrons in that restaurant on that fine Sunday morning, Reader, I do apologize. Normally, we are pretty decent people.

After a crazy meal like that, we needed to walk it off. Traveling to the very west end of Lower Manhattan took us off the main streets and immediately adjacent to the harbor. Everything looked pleasant-- the buildings, the construction barricades, the people on the street, the garbage. After many blocks, the morning's adrenaline took its toll, and we needed our naps. Back at the pad we claimed our beds and couches and dropped into Sunday afternoon slumbers. Only when the Stormtracker called were we roused. "Hi, kids. Now Hurricane (insert current ethnically trendy name) is only four miles from…."

Hours later our merry band gathered for one more excursion. One subway train, ten feet, and fifty toes led us to a tiny Polish restaurant. This time we were far more subdued, which was a good thing, considering how severe the hostess and waitresses looked. Had we behaved the way we did that morning, they probably would have pounded us, Eastern European style.

Surveying the room, my attention was soon drawn away from the women to the busboys-- one in particular. The tall, thin, light brown haired boy was about nineteen or so. He had nicely shaped cheekbones and penetrating eyes, with a quiet sort of demeanor. *I am not checking this kid out or anything, but I cannot stop staring at him. There's something very--* "Oh my God!" Michelle interrupted my thoughts, "Look! It's Daver[*] Junior!" Of course! This kid looked like Senator of twenty years ago. Curiouser and curiouser. Like the reliable and supportive friends that we are, we wasted no time launching into the Son-of-Senator jokes. "So, Daver, where were you, roughly nineteen years and nine months ago?" "No, Baby, I've never thought of adopting a teenager. Why do you ask?" "He's probably just working here until he becomes a rock star."

When we had exhausted our latest cheap comedic material, we walked to the real entertainment. Arturo O'Farrill, son of the late Chico O'Farrill and heir to his Latin jazz band, was playing with his full entourage at a nearby club. The beautiful art deco candlelit room was easily set ablaze from the first number. The concert ran almost and hour and a half, and it smoked from beginning to end. O'Farrill was in control the whole time, and having fun during every minute of it. The solos were sizzling, popping out one after another. A troupe of salsa dancers would not have commanded more attention. What else can I say? If I were one of those writers who still labored under the delusion that 'orgasmic' was a cute adjective, I might use it here. Thankfully, I am not one of those writers.

Not much could top O'Farrill's performance, and our trip was drawing to a close. Monday morning we said our early goodbyes to our friends as they left for work on yet another rainy day. Even Farnsworth had left us. We prepared for a last march up and down Broadway. When the raindrops got heavier, we found bookstores to run into. When the clouds broke, we went back outside and found people to run into.

---

[*] yet another of Senator's names, under which he writes, records, and, every decade or so, usually against his wishes, performs

Our motivation was draining. Gradually, we were ready for home. Returning to the apartment, we gathered our things, had a quick bite to eat, and sat looking at the clock. Somewhere, while running around in the dampness, I had picked up a nifty sore throat and a little congestion, and I wanted to go be whiny in my own bed. Senator phoned the airline. When we became uncharacteristically excited at the prospect of taking an earlier flight out, we knew it was time to go.

On the flight home it occurred to me that this trip had not really been planned out. Correction: the trip was quite planned out; it was just planned out in New Orleans instead of New York. At least we went somewhere with 'new' in the title. Strangely, for about two months prior, I had been craving New York walks. There was nothing in particular I wanted to see. I just wanted to be there, plodding down the streets of Manhattan. When I mentioned this to Senator, he told me he had experienced the same gentle nagging a few times as well. Once again, it seemed that we ended up in the right place at the right time.

Chapter 2
Thousands of Miles, Hundreds of Feet, and Dozens of Degrees: Mid-February 2006

Once we got back from New York, the holidays came and went quickly, complete with feasting, hibernating, and the inevitable acquisition of a slight Midwestern 'winter coat'*. The new year rolled around, devoid of any real differentiation from the old one. The weather had promised ample snow early in December, then gradually gave up and slipped apathetically into that dirty, chilly-but-not-crisply-cold ugliness that is commonly reserved for March. Only once did we get out to play in the snow. In short, the winter, which I usually love, was a bust, and it was time to move on.

My grandma, Dorothy, who spends the colder months in Florida, had given us an open invitation to come and visit her some time. I also had a grandfather living in Florida, just an hour from her. Thus far it had not worked out with our schedule

---
*a polite term for fat

to go to Florida, but now the lure of unused vacation time and the prospect of a road trip to the tropics combined to start us packing. All we needed to do was notify the elated grandparents, get through January, and rub on the sunblock.

Senator often jokingly quotes, in his best smug voice (which is never convincing), that, "If you fail to plan, you plan to fail." Typically, this is good advice. In fact, it has even carried me through college, home ownership, financial investments, and other such adultish things. When it comes to travel, though, no amount of planning ever seems to protect us from some ridiculous and unforeseen occurrence. By this time we had pretty much come to expect this, so it became a beat-the-system game: Senator and Wendy vs. Murphy of the 'law' fame.

Consequently, I cannot say that I was all that surprised when, eight days before takeoff, I opened the mail to find a perky, patriotic envelope summoning Senator to that highest of human callings, jury duty. Naturally, he was to serve while we were supposed to be on vacation. *You have got to be kidding me.* The obnoxious blue ink notified Senator of his chosen status as if he had won some sort of sweepstakes. *Maybe they'll pay him his $10 in a giant cardboard check.* The obnoxious threatening red ink informed him that his privileged position was not optional. No phone calls please. So now what? I was getting sick of asking that question.

Immediately my devious, anarchical mind began to conjure a letter describing physical ailments, religious practices, and personal prejudices that would support the case of Senator going to Florida instead of a jury box.[*] He took a more honorable approach. With the faith of a child and the determination of a man who, for weeks, had been anticipating falling asleep on a

---

[*] I once swayed the Holy Jury Commission from choosing me using one simple statement: I believe everyone is guilty until proven innocent. Feel free to use that one.

beach and not in a courtroom, he called the tiny printed very-special-cases-only-and-screw-the-rest-of-you phone number listed at the bottom of the page.

A pleasant senior citizen's voice answered. Senator casually stated that he had a previous commitment and, most regretfully, would not be able to grace the scales of justice with his presence.

"No, problem. Will you be available a few weeks after that?... Okay, we'll just send a new form out."

He smiled, thanked her, and set the phone down in triumph. Amazing! I guess I had forgotten that we now lived in a small town, in a small county that does things differently, and with far less aggression than our previous hometown. We were free to hit the road.

The funny thing about the Murphy's Law game is that there can be 'false rounds' that play you for a fool. These are minor inconveniences that, due to their easily-resolvable nature, do not count as the true pre-vacation disaster. This we learned the hard way, when, two nights before we were supposed to depart, I walked out from work to find my truck battery dead. Of course, the truck was the intended method of transportation to Florida, as I am not coordinated enough to drive Senator's stick shift. Considering the battery was only about six weeks old, I knew I was in for complicated problems.

With a substantial jump from my employer's car, I tootled my way homeward, racking my brain to construct a Plan B in the next twenty-four hours. My better half calmed down his pacing and incredulous girlfriend and made the necessary phone calls. The next day we dropped off Trucky at our mechanic's garage and made an internet reservation for a rental car. *I knew getting out of jury duty was too easy.*

Friday morning we were at the rental agency early. The day was sunny and traffic was not too bad. I was in a considerably better mood as Senator filled out the paperwork.

The non-secret agent read him the rental agreement and insurance blah blah blah. Finally, she asked Senator if anyone else would be driving the car. I said that I would be driving as well.

"Okay, that will be an extra $55.00."

"All right. Then I'm *not* a driver."

She smiled knowingly. "Well, just so you know, if the car gets pulled over for any reason and you're driving, it will be considered stolen and you will be prosecuted."

"Don't worry," I assured her, "I wouldn't dream of violating our policy."

We took the keys and I climbed into the driver's side. This was getting exciting. Not only were we traveling in a new car, but now I was going to be a potential felon for the next ten days. I imagined myself being booked for 'stealing' the car from my boyfriend, who had legally rented it, and happened to be in the passenger seat at the time. *Hey, would that make me a kidnapper too?*

We started south and east on our merry way. As the hours passed, we watched the outside temperature slowly climb. By early evening we were in Tennessee, where all the radio stations warned of an approaching blizzard. The predicted whiteout would bring "up to two inches"! At home this would have been laughable, barely an excuse to arrive at work a few minutes late. In the South, however, they are not equipped to deal with even a half inch of snow on the highways. While we knew that *we* could drive through it safely, we were not so confident in the abilities of the natives on the road. We quickly agreed that the best strategy would be to continue far enough south to outrun the snow.

By 8:00pm we had gone far enough to be out of the path of upheaval, so we began to look for an exit with accommodations. In Forsyth, Georgia, we saw several signs advertising hotels in the $30.00 range. Though suspiciously cheap, I reasoned that they couldn't all be dives, so we scoped one out. The beehived desk attendant was on the phone with her daughter, who lived 'up north' in West Virginia. The big blizzard was the urgent topic.

"Hold on, Honey, I got me some noss kids here awaitin'...." "Hah, ya'll!" she greeted us, "Did ya'll get snowed on?" We shook our heads and requested a room, our Yankee accents revealing our familiarity with snow. "Oh, well, then, ya'll are used to this sorta thang. Here's ya' key an' ya' t.v. remote. Let's see he-yah… That'll be $28.42. Enjoy now!"

I waited until we were out of her earshot before I laughed. As they say, it is all about location, location, location. Thirty bucks got us a modest, somewhat ugly, but sufficiently clean and bug-free room. In New York thirty bucks would have bribed the desk attendant to *find* us an available room.

Saturday morning we were eager to get back on the road. I again threw my grand theft auto caution to the wind, and climbed behind the wheel. When crossing the Florida border on I-75, it is traditional to stop at the most hospitable welcome center in the country. Informative workers direct travelers to brochures, locate places on the giant wall map, and cheerfully answer questions. The real gem, though, is the person at the juice counter. In one of its finest efforts to suck up to the tourists, Florida passes out fresh squeezed orange juice… FREE! The sticky juice lady participates in an endless cycle of feeding the spinning juicer one orange half after another. An army of filled paper cups is continuously consumed by man, woman, and child as they anticipate their immersion into the Sunshine State.

By mid-afternoon we made the switch from the general interstate map to the specific St. Petersburg map. Though still cool for Florida (low-60s), it was getting exciting. We crossed the miles-long bridge to St. Pete's and followed the directions to Grandma's home. Approaching the gate to the community where she lived, we gave our names, ranks, and serial numbers to the easygoing guard. He waved us through and we drove past the pool, the courts, and many swaying palms visited by beautiful tropical birds.

Turning past the canal inlet, we came to Grandma's place. No matter how old you are, and even if you have stolen a rental car to come see her, Grandma is always ready for your visit with hugs, a big smile, and plenty of snacks. The rest of the day was passed visiting, trading stories, and watching the water. After dinner we sprawled out on the living room floor like, well, like two kids in the comfort of Grandma's house, to map out the week that we knew would fly by.

One thing Senator and I inherited from our mothers is the love of a good bargain. Where better to find good deals and cheap entertainment than at the flea market? Sunday morning we packed Grandma and our cash and headed for the magic of Wagon Wheel Flea Market. The weather was uncharacteristically cold and windy, and it was amusing to see the Floridians in their dusty, outdated winter coats. We pressed our way in and out of the various tents, rejecting the big belt buckles, waffle irons, and stuffed kittens in favor of garden tomatoes, books, organic bug killer (ironic?), and our greatest treasure, the batteryless flashlight. This neat little gadget gets its power when you shake it a few times, emitting a blue violet light, (perfect for the home, office, garage, or car). *We* acquired all this ingenuity for only two dollars, although some poor suckers were paying three dollars for the same item, just a few rows over. Leaving the grand bazaar with loot in tow, we searched out the car in the large, grassy field.

The afternoon was free, giving us time to get ready for the big visit with Senator's old acquaintance, Pat, that evening. Permit me to give a little history here. Back in the early 1970s, the face of the Joliet, Illinois, music scene was rocked by the likes of the west side's teenage sextet, Northwest Ariel. NWA, as they were known long before the rap group by the same initials existed, included a lanky, easygoing guitar player named Pat. Years later, in his late teens, Senator played with him in a different band. Among the other members of NWA was a serious, torn-shirt guitarist named Jim. Jim's lone and faithful groupie, Mary, often attended their garage and basement practices. I was born quite a while after the band disbanded, but I shall ever be a fan, as Jim and Mary later became my parents.[*]

Senator and I never would have been aware of the connection, save one fateful phone call. A few years ago, Senator called Pat just to say hello and catch up on old times. At one point in their conversation, Senator mentioned his girlfriend. Pat asked my name, and for whatever reason, Senator gave my full name, instead of just saying "Wendy". Valkovich, not exactly your everyday good Irish name, piqued Pat's curiosity, and he began asking further questions. I heard only bits and pieces of Senator's answers, and my only concern was why in the world my boyfriend was giving some stranger details about my family history. Frankly, I was getting a bit annoyed. Then he explained everything. His friend Pat, whom I had never met, was my dad's former band mate. Small world indeed! Coincidences like this are numerous and uncanny when you grow up in Joliet, though it hardly qualifies as a 'small town', with its population of 120,000. That's okay; just as long as Senator and I are not related anywhere along the chain of our fair prisontown.

Getting back to Florida, Pat and his wife, Camille, lived just an hour and a half north of Grandma's, so we planned a visit. As it was a Sunday night, Pat and Camille would be playing in their church's worship band, and eagerly invited us to come along. Either way, we would have plenty of time to visit, so I was leaning toward skipping the church part. Though I

---

[*] So now you know what the 'V' stands for. My parents tell the story of how, at their wedding, the band chipped in to present them with a gift of money. The single card contained six dollars... and some change.

have a deep faith in God, I do not have a deep faith in institutions, and I really hate to be the conspicuous 'new visitor'. Senator shares my sentiments, but he also wanted to see Pat play, so off to church we went, in our jeans.

I prayed it would be an old gothic building with lots of stained glass, to add some interest to the experience. Alternatively, maybe they would think I was a kid, and I could go hang out with the youth group instead. I missed on both accounts, but at least the scene was casual. The service was held in a reception hall of the church, with folding chairs around tables instead of pews. Most people were in jeans, like us, and a few had beverages. There was no stained glass in the modern room, but the sunset streamed through the windows. We were greeted by a few friendly seniors, and urged to fill out a name tag to wear, since we were FIRST TIME VISITORS. I thought about writing 'Mary Magdalene', but I try to behave when I make *first* impressions, so I settled on 'Wendy'.

We scanned the room for some nice seats near the back, but our friends quickly intercepted us. They had saved a couple of seats for us at the very front and center table. Great. How was I supposed to take my cue of when to sit or stand or kneel or hold hands or high five, if the rest of the congregation was behind me? *Oh, well. If we embarrass anybody, at least we live 1200 miles away.*

Things eased up a bit when the service started. When we sang songs, the words were posted on the screen in front. When the pastor spoke, he only glanced at us as often as was necessary in an all-around room survey. When it came time to greet each other, no one tried to greet us "with an holy kiss", or anything weird like that. They did, however, seem a little deflated when we announced that we were only there on vacation. I guess that gets us out of usher duty, huh?

Church drew to a close and we accompanied the couple home for pizza, lots of laughs, and a romp down memory lane encircling the glory days of Northwest Ariel. They were warm and hospitable, and the experience had a sweetly surreal feel for me, as though I was witnessing a piece of my own history. Saying our goodbyes at 11:30 that night, we cranked the heat for the ride back to Grandma's house. The Florida temperature had plummeted to 33ºF!

Monday morning's sun struggled to bring the temperature up a few decades, but there was still a cool breeze. No one would be cracking out the swimsuits anytime that day. The main activity, I must admit, had me slightly anxious, though. Senator would meet my Grandpa Al and his wife for the first time. It's not that I was nervous about Senator not getting along with anyone; it's just that my grandpa is not known for his subtlety. His opinions are not hidden behind any shy exterior. Still, he is a sweet and hospitable man, and Senator has a reserved classiness and sense of humor that carries him through just about any social situation, so I had nothing to fear.

In fact, ten minutes into the hugs and greetings, they were trading stories. Again, you have to remember that everyone from old school Joliet knows at least one generation of everyone else's family. The common neighborhood on the east side of town was a blend of Polish and Czechoslovakian immigrants and first-generationers. In short, we are not Mayflower people. My grandpa grew up a block from Senator's dad. He also remembered Senator's mom, as well as various aunts, uncles, and grandparents.

The hub of the Joliet Eastern-European stock was twofold: St. Cyril's Catholic Church and the infamous Eastside Club. Hardworking, blue-collar men spent their brief and precious leisure time making holy confessions in the church and raising holy hell in the club. Senator's mom recalls a New Year's Eve date when his dad took her to the club and someone started shooting the numbers on the wall clock. She immediately demanded they get out of there. When Senator told this story to

Grandpa Al, he was neither shocked nor appalled. He simply responded with a twinkle in his eye, "Oh, yeah. I remember that. That was Fritz. He was a good shot!"

The afternoon was very pleasant, and we were introduced us to a wonderful Italian restaurant near their home in Sarasota. We all ordered, nibbling on the home baked bread in between words. When Senator and I gave our meatless orders, I fully expected to receive a lecture on the values of dead animals in our bodies, but instead, Grandpa just commented that it was good that we enjoyed our veggies. Either he had mellowed out since I last saw him, or I was just someone who worried too much about silly things. I will let you decide.

Our wonderful meal left us satiated beyond comfort. We drove around town for a bit and returned to their home, where we traded more stories. Though we were all still full, we squeezed in some homemade pie and coffee... just to be nice... and because it was irresistible. Sometimes it's just good to be the kids. The day could not have gone better. As we left, Grandpa again told me how much he liked Senator, and how much Senator resembled his father in looks and character. These were high compliments. What a pleasant and fitting end to a day I will cherish for the rest of my life.

Tuesday was our first unplanned day. The weather was warming up a bit, despite the fact that I was not able to check the Weather Channel for confirmation. Barely awake, I presented Senator with a homemade Valentine's Day card, and he gave me a much-cherished Bon Jovi cd, bless his heart. This was pretty much our only concession to the Hallmark holiday. We dressed and made our barefooted way to the porch to ease into the morning with a couple of good books and a bowl of Florida fruit. The porch is literally steps away from an inlet of Tampa Bay, a subset of the Gulf of Mexico. Venturing through the tiny yard and out onto the dock, you might be lucky enough to see some exotic critters. There's usually a heron or pelican hanging around, while chameleons dart around the rocks. Occasionally, a manatee is spotted. The noisiest of all the wildlife, however, may be The Golfer, whose faint swears and errant balls sometimes soar out across the canal when the wind is wrong.

When we achieved a sufficient amount of motivation, I suggested the traditional St. Petersburg outing to The Pier (actual name). The Pier, in case you couldn't guess, is a five-story tourist trap jutting out into the bay from the center of the downtown area. The highest level is the largest, successively getting smaller to its first-floor base. From the shore it looks as though a giant uprooted an ancient ziggurat and threw it into the air, landing it upside-down on the earth. Nevertheless, it is an attractive centerpiece to the city, offering all the overpriced tee shirts and junk food you could want, to accompany your gorgeous view and piped-in Jimmy Buffett music. If you are ever in St. Pete's, trot on down to The Pier, forgive the city's lack of creativity in choosing a name for it, and enjoy the walk, the view, and the fact that you are on vacation and have nothing better to do than make bets as to whether the fisherman below you will get crapped on by the sea gulls that eagerly await their free fish.

Exiting the downtown, we headed west across the county peninsula. No trip is complete if we do not stop at a music store or two. In my role as She Who Plans and Navigates, I scope the yellow pages of our destinations online before leaving home in order to find such places. This time I scanned the listings, selected two, and rejected one, based solely on its claim to fame that, "This store is so cool that Billy Corgan reportedly shopped here in the early 90s!" I kid you not. I can't make this stuff up.

We battled traffic for a while and arrived at the first store. *Hhmmm. Looks a little rough.* I suggested we try the other one, only a block or so away. When we came to the second store, we gave each other one of those looks that couples who have been together long enough use to convey five minutes of conversation in a single glance. Skull posters, tie-dyed panels, and low-budget weaponry filled the window displays, accented nicely with pipes a-plenty.

By now I'm sure you realize that Grandma is quite a hip gal. In fact, her only mission as we perused the junk shops throughout the week was to find a cute toe ring or two for herself. Let's face it though-- this place was a total head shop, and I was not about to subject my sweet grandma to some dreadlocked dropout peddling homemade incense. The only problem was that I knew Senator could find something of value here. In years of managing and shopping record stores, he has fine-tuned the art of combing through such places with the miraculous result of finding rare and often investment-wise cds.

Then inspiration struck, in the form of the retail chain. I had vaguely remembered seeing a listing for a Barnes & Noble nearby. We synchronized our watches and dropped Senator off to fend for himself for a while. I climbed over to my illegal position behind the wheel. With a quick kiss I told him that if we were not back in an hour and a half, he should assume I was hauled off for car thievin', along with my new accomplice, Hot Rod Dot. Without incident, Grandma and I lazed around the bookstore, and later met Senator with his latest acquired gems.

The afternoon was ebbing away, and it was high time we looked for a beach to view the sunset. Fortunately, we were on the correct side of the peninsula. Unfortunately, so was the rest of rush hour traffic. I was just beginning to have my doubts about arriving anywhere before dark, when we came to Redington Beach. The temperature was dropping again, but we only needed to fight the chill for the last ten minutes of sunlight in the day. The timing was perfect. *All right—bring on the pizza and Yahtzee!*

It is probably no secret that this particular vacation appealed to the homey, easily entertained part of us. We did not attend any concerts, or experience any 'night life', save a late night walk around the park. We would not have changed a thing, but everything was so comfortable that I found myself partaking in something I said I never would: the viewing of *American Idol*. As much as the show would annoy me at any other point in time, it was far more entertaining when watching it with Grandma. She updated us on who was who, who could really sing and who stunk, and who was just there to boost the show's ratings. We made fun of the gaudily attired, yelled at the off-key, and laughed at the pompous who got the boot after all their bragging. Please understand, Reader, we are not mean-spirited; we just appreciate the ridiculous.

Another day, another few degrees warmer. Whatever the temperature, it still beat anything February in Illinois could offer. We again nibbled our fruit while watching the passing heron, as he made his morning surveillance rounds. When the spirit moved us, we joined Grandma for a long walk through her community, which, though it has an official name, the locals refer to simply as, The Park. Apparently St. Petersburg isn't too big on vague nomenclatures.

I say it was a long walk, not because of the distance, (although we did put in a good two miles or so,) but because of the social aspect. Either everyone in The Park is very friendly, or everyone just knows Grandma. Both are equally possible. We met neighbors, landscapers, security guards, and a pooch or two. In between greetings, Grandma fulfilled her role as tour guide, taking us past the courts, through the clubhouse, around the pool, by the memorial flower garden, and down the various streets. If you ever want to feel like a celebrity for a day, have Grandma take you around. Everyone stopped what they were doing to say hello and apologize for the 'cold' 70ºF weather, as if it was their fault. *That's right—don't let it happen again!*

It never ceases to amaze me how, when on vacation, I can manage to lie around or nap after only being up a few hours. If this were the case at home, I would never get anything done, let alone write. {buy my book buy my book buy my book} Slathered in sunscreen, I stretched out across the dock with my $2 flea market book. Senator was reclined on the porch, across from Grandma, who was reading the paper. We were a really productive bunch. Hearing a voice, I looked up to see the next-door neighbor emerging with a pot and a box.

Isabel was from Nova Scotia, and wintered among the other Yankees in Florida. She saw that Grandma had company, and took it upon herself to make homemade spaghetti sauce for us. I love Canadians. In her words, she saw us, "eating fruit oot there the other day, and figured we were into healthy food, eh, so there's a lot of vegetables in the sauce." She even brought a box of whole wheat pasta. We thanked her, and were just aboot to grab the pot, eh, when she added, "There's meat in there, too, so I hope you're not vegetarians." D'oh!

She could tell by our grins. "Actually, we are, but thank you so much!"

"Ah, you can cheat for one day!" she reasoned.

We thanked her again, and gabbed away about our families, local attractions, and the beautiful rolling green hills of Nova Scotia, where I plan to go on another trip someday.

Eventually the lazy day led us to lupper[*] in the screen room. We were in the middle of chomping on our big sandwiches and chips when we heard a very loud bang/thud. It sounded almost like something had landed on the roof of the porch, but we had not seen anything come soaring overhead. The tin roof could have echoed a sound from elsewhere. We brainstormed ideas for what could have happened. Maybe something big had been dropped by the neighbors, who were renovating their place. Perhaps there was an explosion. Maybe aliens were finally invading, and they chose a retirement community in the belief that seniors would have gained more of

---

[*] a mid-afternoon meal. makes sense, doesn't it?

Earth's knowledge during their lifetime, would have more leisure time in which to share it, and would be committed if they tried to tell anyone what happened. (It was just a working theory.)

Now all of the neighbors were outside, and we could see news helicopters in the sky. Through The Park's healthy and fertile grapevine, we learned everything we needed to know. Half a mile away, a van was parked for the afternoon, with oily rags lying in the back. The sun heated the vehicle up inside until the whole mess combusted, exploding and blowing out the windows of several apartment buildings. *Well that's something that doesn't happen everyday.* Fortunately, no one was seriously injured.

When things settled down, we left for an evening walk through Sawgrass County Park. The county parks in Pinellas County are better than many state parks I have been to. This particular one features a long boardwalk through the swamplands, and, yes, there are gators there. We only saw a young one, about six or seven feet long. More entertaining than the alligator, who did his best log impression, was the pair of charging armadillos. There is something inherently amusing about watching two round, fat critters run at each other and smack armor like miniature jousters. Often they would hit hard enough to send one up into the air and over the other's back. Who knows? Maybe they were actually courting rather than fighting, but how do you tell a male armadillo from a female?

The sun began to set and we were kindly directed to the park's exit by the ranger. We drove back to Grandma's for the next installment of relaxation. We ambled between stories of Grandma's childhood, reading, and bad *American Idol* performances. So far we had done a lot of nothing, enjoying friends, family, and Florida for what they were. The next day we would be regular tourists, though, standing in line at Busch

Gardens. In the meantime, we were forced to eat fresh strawberry shortcake before retiring for the evening.

Thursday was the day made for us. The weather was warm but not hot, sunny but not glaring. As we left Grandma's to drive to Tampa Bay, we discovered a German bakery, filled with appetizing pastries, plenty of freshly brewed coffee, and some old Germans at a corner table thrown in for good measure. Now we were sufficiently sugared and caffeined for the amusement park. Incidentally, we never consume as much sugar at home as we do on vacation. Perhaps this is related to all of the lying around we do on vacation. I should do a study on it some time.

When we arrived at the park (as opposed to The Park,) we chose one of the eight lines of traffic moving toward the parking lot. When we drove up to the little window to pay to park, the attendant's register or magic machine was not working, so she waved us through anyway. The parking lot was nice and open, and this was pretty much how the whole day went. We walked onto every ride with a maximum of only a five minute wait. The only crowded place was the free beer line, which held no interest for us. I briefly considered trying to sell our free beer coupons, but I suppose that would have been discouraged, and I would hate to have gotten us thrown out for scalping. Nevertheless, the universe was cooperating nicely.

A day at Busch Gardens is a trifecta of activities. There are many species of native African animals to view in their spacious, if not exactly natural, habitats. Then there are the shows. We were fortunate enough to see the latest incarnation of the legendary Les Brown orchestra. Sure, we were swingin' along with the rest of the audience, the majority of which were old enough to be our grandparents. You know us well enough by now.

The final leg of the Busch Gardens experience consists of the world-class roller coasters. In Chicagoland, teenagers frequent the Six Flags Great America theme park to get their fill of loops, dives, twists, turns, and drops, and I was no exception when I was a kid. From my mother I inherited the love of speeding coasters, with the exception of the head-and-neck-rattling wooden coasters. I invite the purists to debate me, but those are just masochistic.

Anyway, Busch Gardens hosts only six or eight large rides, but they are worth the trip. We rode several, often walking on without waiting in line, before Senator decided that they no longer held the appeal they once did for him. There goes my roller coaster buddy. I was okay with this, but there was one more that I still needed to try out. I wound my way through the turnstiles to get on Sheikra. The ride began its ominously slow climb 200 feet up. The anticipation was delicious. The ascent climaxed, and we gradually rounded a turn before the sudden 90-degree drop—which lasted a fraction of a second. On the way down, the ride stops you, suspended in mid-air, facing the long trail directly down to the ground. After what felt like ten minutes, but was really about two seconds, we continued the descent, splashing through water and supposedly hitting 70 miles per hour. YES!

When I had had my fill of twists and turns, we shared some theme-park-priced pizza. Walking past the beautiful gardens, we boarded the tired people's train to ride back across the park. Apparently, it was getting close to closing time. Our railway moved us about a fourth of the distance that we wanted to go, then promptly shut down and wished us a good evening. Shrugging it off, we strolled to the gate, out to the parking lot, and into Senator's rented/my stolen car. It was a gorgeous day, and the atmosphere was far more enjoyable than the over-marketed and brat-infested Disney World. If you get the chance, get your discounted tickets on the internet and go.

Naturally, the evening passed far too quickly, leaving us with only one more day in this particular paradise. After stalling a week, the weather had grudgingly warmed up enough to go swimming. As I mentioned, The Park had a lovely pool, complete with a view of an ancient tree and several boats in the small marina. We did not waste time in donning our swimwear to take advantage of the situation. The pool was not crowded, but to say we stood out would be an understatement. For one thing, we were under sixty-five. Secondly, we were the only individuals for miles around with enough hair to put into ponytails. Thirdly, we obviously could not participate in any of the local gossip. The spectators viewed us somewhat suspiciously, as they went on with their agenda.

"Did she tell you about her son? You know, the one that stayed here last week?"

"No, but I could tell there was going to be trouble… ever since the funeral last January."

"Well, I don't want to be the one to spill the beans, but…"

Don't mind us. We're just two vacationing kids who cannot hear you. We are here to actually swim, not just stand in one place and flap our jiggly arms while complaining about our ailments. Furthermore, we are pretending that we have the pool to ourselves. Be nice to us or else we will swim naked.

We swam to our hearts' content and walked back to Grandma's, refreshed and hungry. Of course, she was prepared with salads, sandwiches, chips, salsa, cheese, fruit, cookies, cake, and beverages. When we had filled our stomachs with some of the items and refused the rest, she interrogated us to determine if, in fact, we had *really* eaten enough. I don't think she was convinced, but we honestly were stuffed. When she gave up trying to feed us more, we put on our shoes to drive to our next destination. I think she may have brought a snack or two for us, just in case.

Crossing to the west side of the peninsula, we again fought traffic to go to John's Pass. In the category of attracting junk shops (or, *junque shoppes,* as you may prefer) and the customers who shop them, John's Pass takes first prize. The boardwalk is situated along a fisherman's wharf. Surf shops and tee shirt mongers line the two stories of outdoor venues. There are also restaurants and a famous ice cream stand. Okay, I do not know if it is actually famous, but it will forever stay in my mind.

When I was a younger girl, my grandparents once took me there for a nice little ice cream cone along the water. I was just about to enjoy that all-imperative first lick of my mint-chocolate chip flavored treat, when the Red Baron of sea gulls swooped upon my scoop, actually picking up the entire ball and flying away. As soon as the foul fowl realized what he had taken in his evil clutches, he dropped the melty mess, with a dramatic splat. The ice cream was easily replaceable, but in the split-second that I saw him approach, I truly feared for my eyes, flashing back to the Hitchcock masterpiece *The Birds*. Thankfully, the stupid, graceful creature did not blind me.

This time the walk was less violent. We skipped the ice cream, but I kept my eye out (no pun intended) for any kamikaze birds. Winding up our John's Pass experience, we each bought our cheap sweatshirts and looked around a bit more, until it all looked the same. By the time we finished battling cross-town traffic, we had worked up an appetite.

Grandma suggested we go to Cody's, which, ironically, is a steakhouse with plenty of vegetarian options. Everybody wins! Cody's is also a fun place. Once you are seated, your server gives you a bucket of peanuts to crack open, eat, and discard on the floor. It's not that they are the first restaurant to allow customers to do this; it's just that all of the restaurants in the North that used to let you do this, have now caved in to their politically correct lawsuits and banned the practice. Not these guys. Woo-hoo! Peanuts on the floor!

While waiting for your food and throwing your shells on the floor, you also get to experiment artistically via the medium of crayons. Whereas other restaurants bring tiny packets of crayons when they see a party with children, Cody's puts them right on the table, even if the youngest member of the table is in her twenties. I impressed Grandma and Senator with my best stick people portraits. (Grandma was the one with curly hair.) You laugh, Reader, but eventually they joined in. It was rather addictive, but soon the food arrived, forever depriving the world of my great abstract portfolio.

When we were done dining and shell tossing, we went back to Grandma's for a final night in the warmth of the sea air and her hospitality. The last streams of twilight were fading as we watched the heron make his evening inspections. All was quiet and serene. What some might consider a lame vacation spent around older people had been, to us, a pass for basking in the sun, the love, and the wisdom of an amazing and often underappreciated generation. On the practical side, because I know you are all wondering, it worked out just fine staying in the home of a relative, which I also realize is special. Nobody got in each other's way and I had many laughs spending the week with some of my closest friends. When I found myself getting too sentimental, I put myself to bed.

The car was packed the next morning, officially ushering in the last stage of vacation. In addition to the things we brought, we were taking home books, records, and even a small evergreen tree that Grandma had given us. We took a few minutes to enjoy the warm morning. It would have been a perfect day to go back to the pool. I'm sure a few of the poolies were glad to see the punks go, but several neighbors stopped over to say goodbye as though we were longtime friends. It was 81ºF as we hugged Grandma and climbed into the car. I was not feeling like a rebel, so I obediently entered the passenger side.

Saturday's drive was fairly easy and fast (not that we would *ever* dream of speeding). The only thing worth mentioning was the consistent dropping of the thermometer.

Each hour lowered it a few more degrees. Every time we stopped for gas, we adjusted our wardrobe to accommodate the colder climates. The first admission of defeat was losing the sandals in favor of real shoes. Extra layers of clothing followed gradually.

By the time we stopped for the night, we were in western Kentucky, pulling off the exit ramp onto ice-covered roads and a whopping 11ºF. We found a room and brought our necessities in, including the evergreen. *Yes, we always travel with trees. Why do you ask? No, you may not charge us for an extra person. Yes, in fact I am aware that trees live and breathe like us, but it doesn't count.* After braving the cold one more time to find a bite to eat, we put on our kerchiefs and caps and settled our brains for a long winter's nap.

Sunday was sunny and cold, and consequently, invigorating. The only state left to conquer on the way home was Illinois. It is here that I remind you, Reader, to make sure that you have someone fun to travel with if you are ever going to drive through such long and boring states. In fact, turn to the appendix at the back of the book for a list of states that require serious entertainment accompaniment while riding. This is no joke. Every year thousands of Midwesterners lose their lives to highway blasé, hypnotized into oblivion by mile after mile of cornfields speeding past the window.

Fortunately, we survived, pulling in front of Fort Zuchowskovich by mid-afternoon. We unloaded and picked up Senator's car to follow me to the rental place. I was sure this was the time I was going to be pulled over, after driving thousands of miles all week as a felon. As it turned out, none of the feds were on to me, with my stealthy sub-speed limit driving. We dropped off the car successfully, and I entered the familiar surroundings of Senator's car for the ride home. The vacation concluded with a last nap on the couch. The upcoming spring and summer would be busy, and it would be a while before we traveled again, but still in the mode of family heritage and roots, I was already planning a brief overnight excursion to Iowa, of all places.

Chapter 3
Czech, Please:
Mid-June 2006

Upon returning from Florida to the snowless mud of a pre-spring Illinois, we turned our thoughts to the home front. Landscaping projects, weekly odd jobs, concerts, and the occasional Chicago venture took the place of any sizable vacations until fall. Nevertheless, it would be hard not to sneak away, at least briefly, in the interim. Soon, the gears started turning, surveying several overnight potentials.

About a year before, while perusing a travel magazine, I came across a single paragraph advertisement for the National Czech and Slovak Museum and Library in Cedar Rapids, Iowa. The name was longer than the description. As a sucker for both heritage and cultural history, I perked up. I am the candidate for which such places exist. I love odd little museums, and yes, I care deeply what kind of textiles Moravian women were weaving one hundred years ago. Furthermore, you never know when you'll need to be able to identify a Czech Republic Santa Claus, (which we later located in the gift shop). My fever was fueled by the fact that I am ¼ Czechoslovakian. This is certainly not impressive to the purebreds, but as a European mutt of several nationalities,* 25% of anything gives me a sense of kinship.

But how, you may wonder, observant Reader, did I talk Senator into going? Easy—he is half Czech. It is, conveniently, our single common heritage, unless you count growing up in Joliet, which is an underworld unto itself.† He readily agreed, and we started the search for a bed and breakfast to compliment the event.

You may think that a single night excursion is not significant. You may think that it is nothing to write home about, let alone an entire chapter in a travelogue. You may even think that it is small enough of an occasion to escape the watchful eye of our omnipresent friend, Murphy. If you think that, however, you are wrong, as we were. Four days before our leave, while working for an awning company, Senator threw his back out. I might add that this was not the comical television experience of having to spend a half hour walking around bent over while other cracked jokes. This was an excruciating leveling of a guy with a fairly high tolerance for pain. The next day he could barely walk, let alone drive comfortably in a car. As he lay on the couch staring at the ceiling, and debating the temptation of painkillers, I could not imagine how he would be able to ride the three hours to Cedar Rapids.

I inconspicuously checked the cancellation policy for our accommodations, preparing to reschedule. Each day, though, he felt a little better and moved around a little easier. Sunday

---

* At some point in my career as an amateur historian and genealogist, it occurred to me that my father's countries of heritage (Germany, Austria, Italy) invaded those of my mother (Czechoslovakia, England, France). Perhaps it should give the world hope that they have been happily married over thirty years.

†For further reference, see/hear Daver's *Ode to Joliet* on his critically acclaimed 1999 release, *Pop Art*.

morning he announced that he wanted to at least *attempt* to go. I packed the car and reclined his seat back as far as possible, padding it with numerous towels. He climbed in slowly, popped an Art Van Damme cd in the stereo, and we were on our way.

We got onto the interstate. "How's your back?"

"It's not too bad. Thanks for driving. I think this will be fun."

We drove ten miles or so. "How 'bout now?"

"Yeah, I think it's going to be okay. I'll let you know if I need to stop."

The first hour passed. "What about now? Do you need to change positions or anything?"

He smiled tiredly at my concern. "No, my *back's* not really bothering me right now," he teased. What can I say? I get over-nurturing at times. Finally, he had convinced me he would survive the trip, so I changed the subject to the anticipated destination. The museum and the Czech Village waited. My mind wandered (not too far off the road) to images of brightly-costumed ladies dancing down the street while their gentlemen counterparts simultaneously walked goats and played accordions.

Soon we crossed the mighty Mississippi River into Iowa, suddenly placing us in the 'western half' of the country, where the states are big, the populations are small, and the radio stations begin with that strange 'K' instead of 'W'. When you are a kid, there is something mystically foreign about crossing a state line. You never forget your first time. I was six years old and we drove to Wisconsin. I remember thinking that, for one magical millisecond, my parents and the front half of the car were in Wisconsin, while my toddler brother and I were left in Illinois. My next reaction was sheer disappointment at how normal my new surroundings looked. The first mile of Wisconsin could have easily passed for the last mile of Illinois! Ah, bittersweet disillusionment...

We followed the rolling hills into Cedar Rapids, and then followed the crazy streets into the historical district. In addition to multiple one-way streets (bit of an oxymoron, eh?), letters and numbers criss-cross at odd angles, and their flow doesn't necessarily correspond to the alphabet. To make things even more interesting, north or east becomes northeast, and south or west becomes southwest. After cracking their code, we found the neighborhood of our destination. We took it as a good sign that a local church was having a kolać* bake sale.

We turned down the main street in the Czech district. Though cute and exceptionally clean, it looked a bit abandoned. We parked the car and got out to explore. A cold drizzle dampened our clothes, but not our spirits. It was vacation, and we were prepared to explore. Walking down the street, we noticed that a few of the shops did not open until later in the day. That only made the essence of coffee and the colorful display in the window of the OPEN bakery all the more appealing.

Inside the 19th-century shop, someone loved us enough to bring all of the confections of the Old Country to our fingertips. And I do mean our fingertips. *I'll take that, and one of those, and one of those...* The plunder of our first stop amounted to a giant kolać, something that resembled an éclair, only a bit darker in taste, a twisty cinnamon-and-sugar stick, and two very black coffees. The shy and hospitable woman behind the counter proudly wrapped our selections, and humbly asked, in broken English, for the few dollars we owed her.

We sampled, sipped, and shared, peering in the windows of the other shops. At the end of the block, we came to the car, parked in the museum lot. Looking past the back end of the

---

*Czech pastry, flaky like a Danish

museum, we could see the river, which dropped off slightly to a lower elevation under a bridge. Hhmmm. Guess that comprises the 'rapids'. Not quite the Colorado River, but picturesque enough, anyway. We deposited the rest of our sweets in the cooler, then headed up to the museum entrance.

Inside, two blue-blazered guides welcomed us and encouraged us to sign in. They immediately asked about our origins and began telling us about the wonderful history of the Czechs and Slovaks in the area. They were deservedly proud of their heritage. I suddenly felt like an imposter. With our ¼ and ½, we didn't even make up one whole Czech or Slovak between us. This did not seem to bother the kind ladies, though. They gave us our tickets and directed us toward the self-guided walk through the main exhibit.

This section of the museum was impressively constructed. Various displays illustrated the political struggles for independence from various oppressors. Another wall honored the great musical tradition of Czechoslovakian talents. *From Dvorák to Daver*, I giggled to myself. Solid furniture, colorful layered clothing, and everyday items for life on the mountain farms were depicted. Far from lacking in the arts, hand-blown, or more precisely, mouth-blown glass ornaments, vases, and baubles also graced the exhibit.

The other half of the museum was used for rotating exhibits. While we were there, the topic was textiles of Czechoslovakia. Reviewing all of the beautiful dresses, pants, shirts, vests, blankets, and footwear, I have concluded that there must have been a few unspoken rules for these master weavers of southeastern Europe.

Rule #1: Everything must contain at least six colors. White may not be included in these, unless it appears as an underskirt to make fuller an over-skirt of more colors. Also, beige is not a color.

Rule #2: The more beads the better. In fact, if a small child can lift it, you need to add a few more pounds' worth. These, too, should be multicolored, or better yet, mirrored.

Rule #3: When in doubt, be sure to include a few religious symbols. These can be pagan floral motifs, or Christian icons, but a combination of the two is best, to be on the safe side.

Rule #4: Did we mention the importance of red? Representing passion, blood, fertility, and protection, how could you even think about sewing without it?

Rule #5: Don't neglect the shoes/boots. Make 'em sturdy because you need to walk long distances through fields and over rocks. Make 'em fancy because you're Czech!

Rule #6: See Rule #1.

When our tour of the inside of the museum concluded, we walked outside to see the cabin of an early immigrant. The humble abode was a standard two-room cabin, 'updated' at some point to include a stove and a few 'modern' conveniences, such as a desk and lace curtains. The most amusing tale, though, came from outside the cabin. At the museum's outdoor dedication in 1995, President Clinton attended, as co-guest of honor with Václav Havel of the Czech Republic, and Michal Kovác of the Slovak Republic. The weather turned unexpectedly cold and nasty, forcing the unprepared secret servicemen to rummage through the Salvation Army store across the street for extra coats. *Another dignified moment in the Clinton administration.*

Our museum tour was done, and we were ready to hit some more of the spots on the main drag in the Czech Village. We muddled through a few antique stores, finding plenty of amusing items, but nothing of necessity. Another shop sold hundreds of blown-glass trinkets, and the owner eyed us a bit suspiciously when we came in to, obviously, not spend any money on the pricey souvenirs. I don't suppose they like their customers viewing them as a cheap art museum. We moved along the street.

The final stop would have made the entire trip worthwhile, even if we did nothing else. We walked into Bessie's T-Shirt Shop (probably not the actual name), and met, appropriately enough, Bessie. Bessie is 82 years young, and about 82 pounds, soaking wet. Her hands are never idle, her stories are never dull, and she keeps her hair out of the way of both by wrapping the long gray braids up over her head. Born in the United States to Czechoslovakian parents, she has traveled to the family's homeland many times, and currently spends her summers teaching the language to grade school children in Cedar Rapids. Years ago she decided to combine art, business sense, and an unmatched passion for her heritage, by designing and producing Czech and Slovak tee shirts. Designs include flags, old sayings, (in the original tongue, of course,) and even one with the most common Czech or Slovak surnames. If you see one you like, though, you had better snatch it up, as she wisely limits each design to 100 copies.

After much labored debate, we chose two shirts. Once the actual purchase was made, the fun began. We were the only customers on that rainy afternoon, during the last hour that her store was open, and we decided to take advantage of it. So did she. We asked a little about her background, and she opened the floodgates. We learned about her family, and her visits to the Czech Republic, and how the oppression and paranoia of communism sapped the economy and joy of many of the people. We learned that she loves the United States as much as she loves the Czech Republic, and vice-versa, hoping never to have to choose between the two. We learned that groceries are bagged differently in Czechoslovakian markets, and that she was embarrassed to be caught carrying purchased produce in her pockets when she could not figure out the system. And we learned that when she feels she has lived out all of her life, she wants to be released to gracefully move on to the next life, with no regrets from friends or family. We spent an hour of time and gained eighty-two years of wisdom; not bad for the price of a couple of tee shirts. Thanks, Bessie.

Bessie closed up the shop and the rain was still streaming over us as we walked back to the car. Senator eased in, and I checked the screwy street map before crawling into the driver's side. We navigated our way past more numbered and lettered streets, finally turning into what looked like an average suburban neighborhood, circa the 1970s-80s. I failed to see how the beautiful, brick Victorian bed and breakfast on the internet would materialize among such mundane surroundings. Nevertheless, we followed the swirling street according to the map.

I was amazed when we ended up in the driveway of a lovely estate. There, hidden away from the rest of the neighborhood by trees on all four sides, was the home, the carriage house, and a century's worth of fully-blooming gardens. Talk about a hidden treasure! A few geese glanced up at us, uninterested, and waddled back down the path to their pond.

The owner came out to greet us. I halfway expected her to dress the part of a Victorian innkeeper, given the setting, but her jeans brought me back to reality. Opening the door to the carriage house, she led us upstairs to a heavy wooden door, which she unlocked with the original skeleton key. *Nice touch.* Sure, anybody could easily pick their way into the room and rob us blind, but the risk was a small price to pay for authenticity. The second floor attic suite had windows on four sides, allowing the afternoon sun to softly illuminate the bed, the vintage dresser, and the toilet.

We stowed our stuff, and plotted our dinner plans. Of course, ideally, we would dine at a tiny little restaurant, owned by a ninety-year-old Czech couple and run by their descending generations. We would feast on potato pancakes while hearing tales of the Old Country from our plump, aproned hostess. When we could eat no more, she would force another cup of strong coffee on us, beckoning us to return. The ethnic restaurant in the Czech Village, however, was not particularly vegetarian-friendly, sprinkling every dish with bacon pieces, or bathing it in sausage-water. Oh well. Mexican it is!

Switching gears back to the western hemisphere, we had our fill of rice, beans, and cheese enchiladas. Not quite bohemian fare, but delicious nonetheless. We toted our modern, stryrofoamed leftovers back to the comfort of our carriage house. For a while we read and talked, and when that subsided, we fell prey to the t.v. *Only we could live our regular, daily lives t.v.-free, and then succumb while in a 130 year old bedroom.* A stupid award show of no caliber, honoring no one we had ever heard of, was rotated with the Sunday night low-budget murder mystery movie. When we had sufficiently rotted a portion of our brains, we clicked off the beast and concluded our evening.

In June, the sun rises quite early, and certainly quite earlier than this night owl. Why do I share this with you? It is as a public service to innkeepers, hotel managers, and general purveyors of hospitality everywhere. No matter how inviting a chamber looks while basking in the evening's candlelight, it loses its appeal when the untreated (or undertreated—because lace doesn't count!) windows usher in a 5:30am behemoth beam of sunlight. I know you don't want to spoil the view. I know the paned glass is original, and you want to show us our money's worth. But at the crack of dawn, I don't want to see anything but very dark walls, and the faint silhouette of Senator next to me. I pulled a pillow over my head and tried to go back to sleep.

Upon waking up again at a more reasonable hour, we put ourselves together and walked over to the main house for the other half of the bed and breakfast experience. The breakfasts at such establishments cover a wide range of accommodations. Many b&bs host a lavish multicourse spread of fruit, egg dishes, meats, pastries, juices, and coffee. Others tone it down a bit, opting to serve a single, simple plate of one standard dish. Likewise, the breakfasting style varies. Some homes will bring a basket or tray right to your room for private consumption. (These unsocial meals are the preferred method.) More often, though, the guests gather together at a prearranged time, seated at a common table, or at least in the same room. It's a nice concept, but it can provide for the occasional awkward silence, or over-polite smiling.

On this particular morning, we enjoyed our apple cinnamon French toast and fruit in the company of one other couple. Unless the other couple happens to be your good friends, or two people that you have always wanted to interview over breakfast, it is the exactly wrong amount of people at the b&b table. If you are the only couple, it becomes a romantic meal, filled with conversation on topics about which you truly care. Conversely, if there are lots of other couples, you can fade into the mix and let the dominant ones have their fill of offering tourism suggestions, discussing their kids' achievements, or testing their cocktail party small talk.

We met the other couple and politely introduced ourselves. They were friendly, 50ish, and seemingly on familiar terms with the owner. Their daughter was about to get married. *Oh, how nice. Congratulations! I'm happily divorced myself…* Their son, whom they were going to visit, attended college nearby, and was an accomplished band competitor. *That's fabulous. I can play Love Me Tender on the piano, sort of.* Don't get me wrong. There is not one complaint I have against these people. It's just one of those social situations that people encounter, where they have to pretend to be interested in the lives of strangers whom they will never see again.

So we returned the serve. "We're from Illinois. No, not a bad drive at all. No, we don't have any children (*and never want them,* I stifled). We're into books, music, history, travel, and planning our retirement as joint-hermits." Overall, I must admit, it was pleasant, but nothing beats your own blueberry pancakes in the comfort of your own kitchen. Pass the syrup, please.

With more polite goodbyes, and enjoy-your-weekends, we left the home, making our way back into the present via the modern neighborhood. My final Czechoslovakian cultural plans centered on a church and a few graveyards. By this time we had mastered the streets well enough to arrive at destinations with only minimal mistakes. When we got to the church, it was less than amazing. We scraped our way up the steep, worn driveway to the battered parking lot. The structure was small, architecturally average for a 19th century church, and most disappointing of all, locked. Perhaps it contained great treasures inside, or the relics of Iowan saints, but we would just have to leave that to the imagination.

The first graveyard, also on a steep incline, looked more promising. We entered through an ornate gateway, and began the crawl down the oak lined road. We have become fairly adept at performing the quick-browse in cemeteries. Bypassing anything younger than 100 years old, we made our way to the rear section, which housed the remains of the Catholic Old Country. Stones ranged from simple tablets of immigrants, to obelisks of wealthier patrons, to representative memorials such as angels (escorts to heaven), or the chopped tree trunk (life cut short). Almost all of the family names in this section of the graveyard were distinctly Eastern European, as opposed to the newer section, which told of the assimilation of other peoples. No matter what your nationality, chances are, there is a graveyard somewhere that records the coming, prospering, and intermingling of your culture, complete with dates, written in stone.

And what of the second cemetery? We looked for it on the map, missed it once, went back, drove in, got out, and walked around. Yes, it was beautiful and genealogically fascinating, but we were accosted by swarms of bugs everywhere we walked. We tried walking faster, then in the sun, then in the shade. Nothing helped, so we admitted defeat and packed ourselves into the Czechmobile for the ride home.

While extravagant voyages and grand road trips are always exciting, there is something to be said for the small, overnight jaunts to obscure attractions. These are the trips that are easy to fit into one's week, and require minimal preparation and financial commitment. Yet, sometimes they are just enough of a detour to keep life interesting. If you have even the slightest interest in your family heritage, (or even if you are more interested in the 'dirt' than the roots,) I recommend that you find a town or neighborhood where you can soak up a particular culture. Partake of the food, learn the history, visit with the locals, and allow your senses to experience the sights and sounds. And when you return home, don't forget to tell your parents all about it.

Chapter 4
May I Use One of Your 43 Bathrooms?: Late October 2006

As a result of my tenure at Barnes & Noble, I developed two friendships which I still cultivate on a regular basis. The first is that of Senator, easily maintained as we have agreed to go through life together. The second is that of Customer Sherie. Not long after the store opened, I had the bright idea to start a comfortable book group for people who do not have a lot of time to read. Each month's selection would be a book of 200 pages or less. The other stipulation of the 'Under 200 Club' was that you had to be under 200 years old to join. Apparently my clever brilliance went unredeemed by the greater Naperfield public, since the only person who ever came to my book group was Sherie.

As you might imagine, the nature of 'the group' became quite informal, as we got to know each other better. A few years later, she and her husband invited Senator and me to their beach home in North Carolina. Coincidentally and conveniently, I had always wanted to go to North Carolina to see the magnificent Biltmore Estate, and Senator had a friend who lived there (North

Carolina, not Biltmore) as well. Thus, the gears began churning to plan the Carolina n' such vacation.

I wish I could say that this particular trip was the one which broke the pre-vacation disaster streak, but it was far from it. Without going into a lot of detail, I must mention that, two weeks before leaving, Senator lost a dear friend of thirty years to a freak accident. As a worldwide traveler who loved and respected nature, we dedicate this chapter to you, Bill. Hope you are smiling down on us.

As the emotional and physical drain of the funeral subsided somewhat, we tried to get back into the swing of things and get ready for our vacation. The general route would take us southeast to the Carolinas, then north through Virginia, and into Pennsylvania before returning home westward. Naturally, the night before leaving, as we were walking out of a pizza place, the news on the bar television caught our eye. Richmond, Virginia, was experiencing severe flooding. That figures.

We then came home to find a message from one of our moms, asking what route we were taking. I could not imagine why she would care, but whatever. When we called her back, we learned that a sniper had been camped out over I-80 in Indiana, picking off motorists. We double-checked our source via the internet and a few more calls. Of course, we learned that the gunman was still at large. Up to this point we had not completely decided between two routes, but that matter was quickly settled in light of this recent development.

In spite of all of the setbacks, we left on time Saturday morning, loaded down with all of our camping gear, in case the weather cooperated enough for us to camp out. We traveled south through Illinois and crossed into southern Indiana to make our way into Kentucky. In Louisville (LOO-uh-vihl) we would get on I-64 east. While still in Indiana, we saw a sign for exit that linked route "62 to 64". Since construction was everywhere, I thought it was a detour to get on I-64, and instructed my pilot to take it.

A few miles into our shortcut, it occurred to me that we had never crossed the Ohio River, or entered Loouhvihl, for that matter. This was hardly a minor detail. I consulted two different maps and, sure enough, we were on 62—Indiana State Highway 62, as opposed to U.S. Highway 62, which *would* have taken us to I-64. *Son of a Peach!* What fool decided to number two different highways the same when they were a mere four millimeters apart on my map? I felt like an idiot as I sheepishly redirected us to the correct '62 to 64'.

All things considered, we made good time the first day, arriving at our first stop in Asheville, North Carolina, by midevening. Though we had camping reservations, it was pouring and we were tired, so we decided to hotel it. We found a simple chain motel and asked for a room. They had three remaining, each priced at more than we would expect to pay in the heart of New York. Forget it! We checked a few more, but everything was booked solid. I finally asked a desk clerk what was going on. "Well..." he started slowly, "the leaves are turnin'. Oh, and there's the gun show."

As I left the lobby I noticed the huge billboard across the street advertising said extravaganza. My Plan B was to go to the campground where we had originally reserved, and just sleep in the car. Then Senator brought up an excellent point: where would all of these gun-toting hillbillies who couldn't find a hotel room be staying? He is so wise. We drove around until we finally found a vacancy sign.

Indeed, the ugly, outdated, motel was eager to overcharge our desperation. I don't remember the name, but Shame of Calcutta would have worked. We climbed the rickety, metal, slippery, outdoor steps to our chamber of doom. The antiaromatherapy of stale cigarettes hung in the air. The bathroom was dilapidated at best, with its broken floor tiles and barely functional sink. I will say that there were no bugs, presumably because they found better accommodations. Though the room was not actually visibly dirty, it just gave you that filthy feeling. And the television did not even get the Weather Channel.

I could describe the bed, but it is best depicted by telling you that we hauled our sleeping bags in and lay them on top of the bed to minimize any physical contact with the furniture. We turned the television on for distraction. A couple was fighting in the parking lot. We turned up the volume. When it came time to go to sleep, we left the television on for white noise, but there were not many programs to choose from at that hour in the Blue Ridge Mountains. Suffice it to say I vaguely remember a Southern Baptist revival preacher invading my dreams.

Mercifully, morning came. I wanted a shower, hot coffee, and to get to Biltmore. Biltmore Estate is the largest private residence in the United States, built and passed down through generations of Vanderbilts. It has aptly been called one of 'America's castles'.

I got up my courage and stepped into the bathroom to debate a shower. There was no question that I needed one, but this one might make me feel dirtier. I opted to at least try it, turning on the creaky faucet. Cold…cold…still cold. *I can't do it.* I did my best with a sink bath, washing with a cloth from home. Senator then went in to use the toilet, which of course overflowed, through no fault of his own. We left as quickly as possible. I fully expected to find the truck robbed, but thankfully it was alright. The first night is always a little rough, so we tried to have a good attitude and get on with the fun stuff.

Biltmore was only moments away, and as you drive through the downtown Asheville area, most of the businesses resemble the English Tudor architecture of the mansion. This is attractive, but rather absurd when applied to the local McDonald's. We found a bagel shop to regroup and kill time until Biltmore opened. It was still chilly and rainy, but things tend to look better when there is cinnamon involved.

When the estate opened, we drove the 'driveway' for three miles to reach the home. *Heck of a walk to get your mail!* It was, of course, beyond words, but I shall try. Picture an immense four-story English Victorian castle, complete with fountain, gardens, and sculptures, set among hills of smoky autumn-painted trees, as far as the eye can see. (Or just go to their website.)

The entrance places you in a grand hall, adjacent to a glass-domed solarium. From there, you begin your 1½ hour self-guided tour through the four acres of floor space, including galleries and chambers and drawing rooms and servants' quarters, etc. etc. etc. Among the highlights are the dining room, (which almost spans the same length as our home's property, and contains a full cathedral pipe organ,) the observatory, the model room, (complete with dollhouse-scale replica of Biltmore,) and, of course, the forty-three bathrooms.

We had timed it perfectly, though. Arriving early allowed us to beat the crowds, and by the time we got out, the sun was shining. We wandered the acres of gardens for awhile, and then drove to the working farm and winery, located just a few miles away on the same 8,000 acre property.* Overall, it is obviously worth seeing, but be prepared to be ever-so-slightly sickened by the obscenity of wealth contained in this single residence.

Leaving Biltmore in an overwhelmed daze, we drove down to South Carolina. There was no purpose in this whatsoever, other than the fact that it was not too far away, and it would allow us to check one more state off the list of those we had visited together. We crossed the state line, found an exit one mile later, and got back on the interstate to North Carolina.

---

* Through the years the Vanderbilts have sold off bits and pieces of Biltmore's land, scaling it down from its original 125,000 acres.

Senator did not roll his eyes, but I think he may have laughed at me.

It was sunny, but after staying at Hotel Hell the night before, we figured we deserved showers and real beds, so we skipped camping and found a hotel. Not to be robbed of at least some of the camping experience, we found a nearby park and cooked out for dinner. Fall is a great time to picnic and enjoy spacious natural recreation areas. Packing it up, we went back to the hotel for an exquisitely restful evening of books, the Travel Channel, and junky snacks, which, I might add, never count on vacation.

Monday morning's sun presented more opportunities to cook out. Pancakes, eggs, and camp coffee made a few joggers in the local park jealous. When we finished, we drove the short ride to Senator's friend's home. Steven and his wife Tony had recently renovated a Nineteenth Century house to its former glory, right down to the wooden rocking chairs on the porch. The fiery red and orange oaks set it off as the perfect October retreat. Once inside, we were given the full tour, along with introductions to the personalities of their dogs and cats.

Since Steven still had work to do and Tony was not home yet, we left on our own to explore the local Revolutionary War site. The visitor center stood on the grounds of the Battle of Guilford Courthouse. It was a cozy little museum, with many decent artifacts, but the requisite fifteen minute interpretive film almost made me laugh. The battle was presented play by play, via stop-motion rectangles. (We were blue; the illustrious Redcoats were red, get it?) It was a very bloody battle *(aren't they all?)*, but in the end, "the British suffered heavily, losing ¼ of their army, as the Americans proved their resistance". They neglected to mention the apparently insignificant fact that, though they may have proved their resistance, the colonists lost the Battle of Guilford Courthouse! I guess the winners will always write history.

We left the battlefield and went back to Steven's home. It was decided that we would all go to meet his lovely wife for dinner at a local Indian restaurant. This worked well as Senator and I had hoped to treat our hosts to dinner. Steven said he would drive, so I did not need my keys. Unfortunately, my pea brain associated that fact with not needing to bring a purse, either. Somewhere between their house and the restaurant, it occurred to me that we had no money or credit card with us. *How could I be so dumb?* More to the point, how could I break it to Senator? I poked him once or twice from my perch in the back seat. "I forgot my purse."

Before Senator could react to my subtle comment, Steven broke in. "Oh, you don't need it. We're almost there." I tried to think of a graceful way out of this one, but nothing came. I just kept envisioning myself as the Mooch Friend. You know, the one who conveniently forgets his/her wallet when the bill comes. *But I'm not like that! I swear we were planning to buy dinner!* As it turned out, our meal was a lot of fun, and our friends had a great sense of humor about the predicament. And just so you don't think I am a bum, Reader, know that we were able to return the favor.

We spent a fun, late night with Steven and Tony, which I intended to follow with a late-sleeping morning, but there was the sun factor. The multi-windowed guest room pointed me out to the invading sunrise. It was annoying for a moment, but that quickly faded when I realized I was on vacation in a second-story room that felt like a tree house. It really was a gorgeous morning. As long as I could enjoy it from bed I was okay with it.

Soon the pet parade began. One of the dogs nudged his way into our room, which also had a door to the back staircase. He walked past the bed, seemingly in his routine, did a double-take when he noticed us, and strolled over for some attention. Not to be left out, two more critters tried to sneak in, but were busted by Tony, who ushered them out and shut our door.

Again, somehow, one of the dogs got the door open, and waited at the edge of our room while Tony got ready in the adjacent bathroom. The pooch demanded to know why we were in her spot. The perturbed pup glared accusingly at us, the reason her usual route was closed off. It was comical to say the least. I don't believe I have ever interested so many animals. I would not be surprised to find out that they formed a committee to take this houseguest issue up with their humans.

Senator missed the show, slowly awaking to my animal kingdom stories. We got ready and let Steven talk us into a coffee date before departing. Down the road a short distance was Rendezvous, a hip café run by a Frenchman named Julien, who prided himself on his quiches and pastries. The décor was half typical café chic, and half portraits of unknown locals as an advertisement for someone's photography service.

I ordered my small soy latte[*]. At first he accidentally made it with regular milk. No big deal. When I asked for a new one, he was so disgraced by his error that he generously made me a large, apologizing all the while. *Really, it's okay.* I think he felt that he had dishonored France. We then chose our quiches and he told us all of their vital statistics, and why we had made excellent choices.

As we waited to pay, a lady who knew Steven happened to come in. They talked for a moment, then he jawed some more with Julien. As Steven knows, or will eagerly meet, every person in town, it was a fun conversation, and we were welcomed to town countless times by strangers. When the greetings calmed down, we sat and sipped our coffee, lazily thumbing through a used copy of the local paper. "Hhmmm. Looks like your picture, Steven."

"It is. I'm on the town's beautification committee. That's me with the plant and the shovel."

---

[*] Soy latte is people!

"Well I guess that explains your celebrity status. Stinkin' paparazzi!" From that moment on, I dubbed him Citizen Lantz. Apparently the honor was too much for him. He spilled his coffee all over the tiny table and onto the floor. Boy we are a fun bunch to have around! Alas, inevitably our coffees cooled or were consumed, signaling us to say goodbye. It was time to drive to our next destination.

It took about four hours to drive to Sherie's beach house. We followed the interstate down to the coast and crossed over to Oak Island. Its position is unique in that, though on the East Coast, it sits along a ridge of land that curves around to the south. This allows the lucky inhabitants to view both sunrise and sunset over the Atlantic Ocean.

We continued driving along the island, searching for our friends' home among the many colors and styles of beach houses. Once we found it, we parked in the sandy driveway and sat still for a moment before getting out. The ocean was at the edge of the property, and the wind slapped the waves down on the shore. We took our time going to the door, pausing to examine shell fragments and a tiny crab or two.

It was time to see my friend and meet her husband, Mac, for the first time. Though I already felt like I knew him, I had never actually met him. Ironically, Senator had, on several occasions when they came into Barnes & Noble. Once the introductions were made and the so-I-finally-get-to-meet-yous were complete, we settled in quite comfortably. Besides the fact that we all got along socially, I think it helped that we all had the same plan for the few days we were there: have no real plan, and enjoy it all.

Yes, our schedule was rigorous that day. Within moments of arriving, we were on the porch with cups of coffee, watching the dolphins while chatting with our friends. They like to follow the shrimp boats, frolicking with each other and hoping for an easy meal.* Throughout our entire visit we could look out at almost any time and see them there.

The wind continued to whip along the beach wildly, but when Mac and Sherie suggested a walk, we were not about to miss out on a sandy promenade. We bundled up and journeyed toward the island's latest attraction, the turtle nest. Giant sea turtles make nests in the sand, where they lay their dozens of eggs. To protect the eggs, they then cover the whole thing with sand. When it comes time to hatch, the turtlettes peck their way out, and then begin their epic Flop to the Sea. In a perfect National Geographic setting, the moonlight over the water guides them out to the ocean, where they swim happily ever after. In reality, only one or two out of the 100 or so hatchlings actually survive.

Hence, a turtle nest is a source of major news in a beach community. Anyone you meet greets you with, "Seen any hatchlings yet? Should be any day now." When we came upon the celebrated nest, it sort of looked like any other pile of sand, except that someone had raked a smooth path from it to the water's edge, the sea turtle equivalent to the red carpet. To further assist the little guys, the local restaurant/bait shop owner nobly vowed to turn off his lights when the hatching began. Otherwise, turtles often erroneously move toward man-made light, and never reach their destination. It is easy to get caught up in the excitement, however, no turtles emerged during our stay. I was just glad I did not do anything dumb like accidentally step on the only survivor. That would have been bad, and I'm sure I would have been exiled from North Carolina for life.

We were just in time to see the sunset when we got back. It dangled over the water for a few minutes, and then picked up momentum as it dropped. I have watched many sunsets all over

---

* The dolphins, not Mac and Sherie

the country with various friends and family, and in those last few seconds when it is sinking beneath the horizon, no one ever speaks. Somehow everyone recognizes the solemnity of the occasion as a silent prayer of thanksgiving goes up to the Creator of such masterpieces.

Filing back into the house, we inhaled wonderful smells from the oven. In anticipation of our visit, Mac and Sherie brought several vegetarian Mexican dishes home to cook and sample. (To them and others who have taken it upon themselves to share a meatless meal with us, thank you! That is a very thoughtful aspect of hospitality... and I'll bet you didn't even miss the cow.) We ate like Gringo kings and passed the rest of the evening with music, silly stories, and of course, a few more rounds of the bean brew.

Halfway through our trip we still had not camped, but I was doing my best to simulate the certain camp-like experiences I had anticipated. This charade mainly took the form of cooking, so Wednesday morning I checked my arsenal in the cooler to see what was available. By mixing a few items into a batter and twisting six arms, I was able to make apple cinnamon pancakes for my compadres. Before you christen me St. Donna of Reed, I should admit that I let the others clean up my mess, and I am not known for my neatness during the cooking process. Unlike television cooking shows, my ingredients are not lined up in little glass bowls, and there is generally as much flour on me as in the batter.

With our tummies full, we drove around the island viewing the many styles of beach homes. Like anywhere scenic that started out secluded, Oak Island was morphing. Original tenants were selling out, often afraid of hurricanes. Others were moving in, building monster retreats or planting more docks. Still, enough of the land is kept rugged to preserve some fantastic views.

The next item on the lazy agenda was a trip to Town. 'Town' is the sleepy fishing village of Southport. We strolled around a working lighthouse or two, and then went antique browsing. Though I have mentioned how much I detest shopping, antique stores are exempt, probably because they possess such a museum-like quality that I enjoy getting lost in my imagination. Plus, no pushy sixteen year old is telling me how great I'll look in one of their chairs.

I guess technically I shopped, since I bought a pack of votive candles. The clerk did not seem to see the humor in her explanation of the return policy for my $4 candles. I told her I lived in Chicago, and probably would not be returning them. She still didn't laugh. I told you these places were like museums. When was the last time you joked around with a curator?

After antiquing we went for lunch. The shore side restaurant, of course, specialized in seafood dishes, but Sherie quickly turned us on to their real gems: the hush puppies. If you have never encountered a hush puppy, it is a golf ball-sized corn fritter, dipped in thick batter and deep fried with a whole lotta' southern love. Prior to Southport, I had only tasted them from a fast food restaurant in the North, and, needless to say, was unimpressed. In the Carolinas, though, a hush puppy is delicious enough to actually stop a dog (or human) from hollering, hence the name. This is especially true when dipped in their signature honey butter. Formal, no. Decadent, absolutely. Oh, yeah, and we ate some other inconsequential food there, too.

We transitioned from soaking up honey butter to soaking up the local history. The maritime museum in beautiful downtown Southport offered everything that I have come to love about small museums. The lady by the door asked for the couple bucks' admission fee, almost apologetically. The building looked tiny, but it was one of those places that just keeps going once you are inside. Each twist and turn around the self guided tour led to impressive displays. Parts of ships, maps, models, old news clippings, and many shipwrecked items told the story of the wild and dangerous Carolina coast.

Also surprising was the portrayal of Christopher Columbus in the video that they were playing. The documentary, which chronicled the history of pirates in the Americas, named Columbus as the first. Finally, the truth! I am vindicated! I have been preaching this to bored history students for years, and now I have a scratchy VHS video in a bonified maritime museum to back me up.

The sun was moving westward, (unless you are one of those people who believe that the sun stands still and the Earth rotates,) and we had just enough time to get back to Mac and Sherie's porch to watch it set. Again, it perfectly slid down the layers of colored clouds. Again, no one spoke for those last moments. It was a moving experience, and we mused in our inspiration until Mac announced it was time to commence The Scrabble Game.

There are two kinds of families, and no, I don't mean functional and dysfunctional. There are those who train their children in the fine art of the board game, thereby producing intelligent, creative, socially well-adjusted offspring. Then there are those who never care enough to unfold the board of familial devotion. They throw no dice and move no tokens. They cannot even distinguish between the colored denominations of Monopoly money. Sadly, their children generally grow up to be criminals, or worse, politicians. So America, if you want a brighter tomorrow, polish those Scrabble tiles and sort out your Clue weapons. Future generations will thank you.

We claimed the four sides of the board, and drew our tiles. I had been warned that Mac was the reigning Scrabble king, but I felt confident enough that I could at least make him work for the win. After all, board games run in my blood. Heck, my mom and her sister have even invented ways to play long distance games over the phone.

We sported our game faces, and actually, we all played well, but not well enough. Mac was not to abdicate his throne that night. I don't even remember him furrowing his brow in the common stumped-Scrabbler pose. Sherie is a force to be reckoned with as well. The woman drops more xs than a Times Square marquee, and she never wastes them on single or double word scores. No, she lies in wait, and then frugally spends the x on a triple word score, usually intersected by some rare word containing a q, j, and p. As for Senator and all of his talk about how he is terrible at board games, he certainly did no worse than I did. I never had so much fun losing, and it was truly an education. We played late and went to bed, still marveling that 'qi' is a real word.

The time with Mac and Sherie went fast, and we were soon saying goodbye to them and the dolphins. Thursday morning would take us north into Virginia, to Richmond, capitol of the proud Confederate States of America. To preserve their brief history, the CSA established a museum not long after the Civil War/ War Between the States/ War of Northern Aggression ended, and this Yankee-raised girl was looking forward to gaining a southern perspective. At the risk of being stoned in my Land of Lincoln home, I admit to being a southern sympathizer. After all, I would have supported our cause for independence from Britain; so why not the South's independence from us?

The traffic in Richmond was bad, and there was construction all over the downtown. The orange signs directed us to a parking deck for hospital visitors and museum visitors. We circled the dark aisles and parked. We were low on gas, but there were stations not far away, and we were pressed for time, so we decided to get gas afterward.

We entered the museum less than an hour before they closed. I stepped up to the desk to purchase admission passes, and the attendant alone was worth the price. The old man looked like he had somehow gotten lost and had been trying to find his Virginia regiment for the last 140 years. His gray uniform still fit, but his spectacles slid down his nose when he reached for our tickets. He looked at the clock, paused for a moment, and then, in an act of foreign diplomacy toward Billy Yank and his girlfriend, graciously informed us that he would only charge us half price, since it was late. That was an extremely kind gesture. I hope he finds his company someday.

Though not in the greatest neighborhood, the museum itself is high quality. There were portions of uniforms from countless generals, as well as personal artifacts and documents. One room is strictly devoted to the southern art produced in the years immediately following the war. Though the South suffered great casualties in lives and property, the culture was intent on promoting the image of the grand, graceful, and glorified southern gentleman-soldier. Possibly the most striking of all of the exhibits, though, were the various battle flags on display. Seeing a picture of a flag is one thing; seeing a tattered cloth full of bullet holes and dried blood that once served as a beloved patriotic symbol is quite another. Yankee or reb, if you are in the area, please make the stop at the Museum of the Confederacy if you want an out-of-textbook perspective on the Civil War.

The museum closed promptly at six o'clock, and we hurried back to the parking deck. The only problem was that it looked a little different than when we left it. We had not noticed that the door we came out of had a flush back, making it practically indistinguishable from the cement wall. This also meant that there was no handle to open it from the outside. *There must be another way into the stairwell.*

I walked to the other side of the stairwell to look for a door. As it turned out, the door was not necessary, as most of the seven foot window was busted out. We edged our way in, careful not to rip our backs open on the protruding glass. Once inside, it would only be five flights up to our parking level. We were up for a brisk walk, so up we hiked. It was not without its artistic merits, though. Every landing had plenty of graffiti, usually accompanied by the letters 'SSG'. Somehow I didn't think it stood for 'Senator's spirited girlfriend'. At the top, the mystery was revealed when the words, 'sick sad gangsters' were spelled out. *Well there you have it.* Someday that boy is going to learn not to let me navigate our adventures. That day, however, me n' mah homeboy had to press on.

Thankfully, the door at the top opened to our parking level. We quickly got in the car, relocked the door, and started it up. The gas warning light came on. Senator shot me one of those male 'this-just-keeps-getting-better' looks. Oops--forgot about the gas thing. Fear not, though, there is at least one station a mere block or two away.

Driving to the gas station proved itself another challenge. Due to construction detours and one way streets, there was no way to get to it. I remembered seeing another station about a mile or two before we got to the parking deck. The only trick was figuring out exactly where it was among the crazy, twisting ramps and roads.

Fortunately, I was able to get us there, but when we saw the place, I began to wonder if that was a good thing. Generally, we do not stick out too obviously as tourists, but we were in a pretty rough area of town, and already the other fine patrons were staring us down. To add to the ambiance, there were signs everywhere about paying first, and gas thieves being prosecuted to the full extent of the law. Senator chivalrously locked me in the car and pumped the minimal amount of gas to get us out of town. Meanwhile, I played lookout, plotting how I would fend off a gang to save Senator using a half-empty bottle of hairspray and the grill lighter, should the need arise.

Good. We were on our way out of Richmond without incident, back north to the mother land. Overall, the city struck us as dirty, cramped, and lacking the southern romantic image for which it is known. There were definitely some attractive old buildings, but nothing that you could not get in most historic sections of old towns. It is a shame that the once grand city is not better preserved. (I now invite all nasty emails from Richmond residents.)

From Richmond, it is an easy scoot up I-95 through Maryland, D.C., Delaware, and into Pennsylvania. By easy, I mean that you do not have to get off or change roads. This stretch of road still requires plenty of alertness, as normal rush hour times do not apply. Though it was 7:00pm or so, the road was packed from Richmond to Philadelphia. There were few breaks in speed, as everyone kept it moving quickly, but cars filled as many lanes as were available at any given time. *This must be a picnic at about 7:30am on a Tuesday!* Drivers dart in and out, seizing any opportunity to cross over to a necessary lane. In fact, if you are planning to drive in Europe, zipping along I-95 might be the best practice you can get stateside.

You should also be prepared for tunnels. There are several, which are good to break up the monotony, but they can get annoying as you readjust your eyes back and forth from glaring fluorescent lights to the night sky. While you are adjusting your eyes, do not forget to start digging through your wallet or purse for toll money. Don't bother looking in the ashtray; coins will not get you far here. Toll amounts are given in dollars, and the most expensive one we encountered demanded a whopping $7!

Just south of Philadelphia, we stopped off for the night. It had started raining again, and the temperature was decreasing as the wind was increasing. I officially conceded the idea of camping to another vacation at another time in another place. Once settled and changed into warmer clothes, we considered our dinner options. Cooking anything we brought was out at this time of night, and we were too tired of driving to go far, so we opted to slum it at the Denny's across the street. *Oh how the mighty have fallen.* I had not been to a Denny's since I was a kid, and all I remember is that a waitress spilled hot coffee on me. I recovered, she cried, and that was about it, but it was enough to keep me away thus far.

We graciously unfolded our giant plastic menus. At least the food would be hot, and let's be honest: it would be pretty hard to mess up eggs and potatoes. After a half hour, the food came. I must say, it was quite fresh, and satisfyingly steaming. Maybe they have their own chickens, and it took a while to convince them to produce on such a cold, rainy night. We finished eating and chugged our way back to the hotel. It was hard to believe, and a little depressing to realize that we had awoken to a view of the beach that morning, and now viewed a parking lot in a suburb of Philly. Nevertheless, warm, dry sleep came quickly.

Friday morning was still chilly and gray, but not as nasty as the night before. We drove the few miles into downtown Philadelphia, and parked in a deck very different from the one in Richmond. For tourist purposes and national monument security, the historic district is kept neat and carefully guarded. It was a short walk across the square to Independence Hall, but it was enough to get my nose running and my eyes searching for a coffee shop.

When we approached the security guard at the entrance, he asked for our tickets. Tickets! I didn't know anything about needing tickets, and apparently their website did not feel that it warranted mentioning. He explained that tickets were free and readily available, but we had to walk back to the visitor center to get them. I refolded my thinning Kleenex and we hiked back for tickets. This time we returned legitimately and lined up for our tour, careful to avoid the student field trip group.

Once inside, it is hard to believe that the documents which we take for granted as law were formed by a few dozen guys arguing one summer. There was a lot of strategy involved that is often left out of textbooks. I learned that the question of how to present the new laws to the people was a great source of concern. Many could not read, and those who did might not understand the true meaning of these laws and declarations. Then there was the possibility of riots, or mobs attacking the delegates. Even if everyone supported the new government, would it last once things got tough with the British? It is nothing short of a miracle that it ever came together, and that it has worked relatively well so far. On the other hand, as Senator's friend Steven says, "If we had known the British were going to have better comedy than us we wouldn't have declared independence."

Outside Independence Hall is a small building which houses the famed Liberty Bell. We passed by, but did not go inside, as I remember it being a disappointment from when I last saw it as a teenager. In my book, it ranks second only to Plymouth Rock as the Lamest U.S. Historical Attraction. It is a bell with a crack in it. Was it rung when independence was declared? Did it toll as the final treaty was signed, ending the Revolutionary War? Did Ben Franklin gaze upon it as he searched the sky for lightning? Hardly. As a matter of fact, it was made about fifty years after the colonial period. For a while it sat atop a state building, and then it was paraded around the country every so often before returning to Philly. No one knows for sure when it cracked, but historians surmise it was sometime around the middle of the nineteenth century. Boooo.

Our next stop was Franklin Court. This is a small courtyard which leads to an underground museum dedicated to the statesman, philosopher, and inventor. In the yard, there are large beams that are erected to form the outline of his Philadelphia home. To exit the courtyard, one passes through a small post office, where the cancellation mark is a stamp of Franklin's signature. There is no doubt that this man is Philadelphia's favorite son.

From the courtyard we walked a few short blocks to Christ Church. Regardless of the weather, the best way to explore downtown Philadelphia is on foot. Everything is fairly close together, and it allows you to see the federal architecture from various angles. This was especially pleasing when approaching Christ Church.

The congregational meeting place served many of the founding fathers, including the Washingtons when they were in Philadelphia. The outside is surrounded by large old trees, many of whom witnessed the colonial inhabitants. Inside, many of the multipaned windows are original, and the simple wooden pews lead up to a reverent white altar. Alongside the pews are name plates, often reflecting the well-known British heritage of most of its members. Beside serving as a house of worship, the structure was also used as an early communal meetinghouse. Now, over 200 years later, you can still attend church services there.

We left the beautiful church and made our way toward the last of the Philadelphia stops: the historic downtown graveyard. If you have learned anything about my love of history, you remember that graveyards are one of my favorite haunts, no pun intended. Few places are so immediately tactile to my imagination when picturing the past. There is connection, and, as long as it is not an ugly modern cemetery, there is respectable beauty.

As we quickly learned, there is also commercial potential. Ironically, I had just remarked to Senator how wonderful it was that all of these points of interest were free and open to the public. "That's how it should be," I orated, "The People need to have free access to the symbols of their freedom! Education about our heritage must be made available! This is our birthright as citizens and taxpayers!" It was the instant I noticed the booth with the cash box and the guide maps for sale that I slipped off my soapbox.

"You want tickets?" Benedict Arnold asked, "Two dollars for adults." Senator left the moral decision in my lap. True, four dollars is only four dollars, but it was the principle of the matter. Some history whore wanted me to pay to see a sacred burial ground. A donation for upkeep I could see; but to actually *charge*... In the end my curiosity got the best of my ideals, and I admitted defeat. Four singles were plunked down in disgrace, dozens of forefathers rolled over, and we entered the iron gate.

Beyond that, there is not much to tell. We saw the graves of early Philadelphians, including the Franklin family. I enjoyed trying to decipher eroded stones, and made careful note of the different carved symbols. In general it resembled most of the Eighteenth Century graveyards in New England. Yes, it was worth the sacrifice of four dollars, but I will continue to stew over the sacrifice of principles.

The drizzle further continued to taunt us, driving us toward our sole, pathetic revenge. We marched ourselves to a crowded and inviting diner, run by a staff of sprite senior citizens. We opened the door and searched for a couple of seats around the two u-shaped counters. The man behind the register was waving papers and yelling something in Greek. The commotion was not particularly directed at us, so we perched on our stools and grabbed a menu to share from its chrome stand.

In a moment Rita approached. Rita made my 5'1" frame look large, but that did not slow her down. She trounced up to us and gave us a huge, wrinkled smile with brown eyes opened wide in anticipation of two more people she would get to talk to today. "Want some coffee, kids?"

"Yes, please." She poured our coffee, and began to rattle off the specials, interrupting herself to give a few college kids their bill.

"Have you been here before?" We were about to slip in a quick "no", but she went on. "This place is real good. It's owned and run by Greeks. Are you Greek? No, you don't look Greek," she pronounced before we could answer. "That's okay. I'm Italian myself, but they do a real good job here! Now what'll you have, a Philly cheesesteak?"

I briefly wondered if she would process our order, or just bring us whatever she decided we should try. "I'll have an omelet, and she'd like the roasted vegetable pita," Senator ventured, gesturing toward me. (For some reason, most likely due to watching too many black and white movies, I get a kick out of letting Senator order for me. For the record, I also strongly approve of the firm tip-the-head-back-kiss, popularized by Hollywood gents of the 1930s and 40s, but I digress…)

Rita was amiable and continued to interview us about our visit to the city she loved. She seemed to like everyone, but we really won her over by complimenting all of the sites we had just toured. Meeting people like this is always a bonus when on vacation. Because they are eternally pleasant characters who adore their hometowns, they further propel the fantasy that is a vacation. Nothing is ever wrong here. The plumbing is never screwed up, no one works on holidays, and everyone picks up their dog poop when they walk their non-shedding hounds. It all makes the dream a little sweeter.

Soon the food arrived, balanced on Rita's hands, forearms, knees, chin, and shoulders. Okay, it was not quite that acrobatic, but it was still pretty amazing. She lay down item after item. Food was followed by fresh coffee (because she decided that Senator's had sat for too long to be revived simply by topping it off), ketchup, packets of an indistinguishable sauce, extra napkins, straws for water, silverware, and other things I am surely forgetting. She was a capable representative of the City of Brotherly Love.

When she was satisfied with her spread, she turned around in a flash to take someone else's order, yelling it to the kitchen in between. Now let's see if the food lives up to the service. Eating meatless meals can be somewhat limiting when we want to try a regional dish, sometimes forcing us to choose similar substitutes. I figured that a sloppy grilled veggie sandwich was as close to cheesesteak as a vegetarian could come, so I was looking forward to that first hot, juicy bite. You may scoff, Reader, but I would confidently serve this sandwich to any carnivore. Sautéed onions, peppers, mushrooms, broccoli, and tomatoes were dusted with oregano and served inside a hearty toasted pita. It was seasoned perfectly and absolutely delicious, but with enough grease to satisfy even the most anti-healthy eater.

We thanked Rita in speech and tip. I hoped that she would not have to keep waiting tables for too many more years. On the other hand, maybe a job like this is what keeps someone like her going strong. We zipped our jackets up and opened the door against the wind and rain, stepping our gait up for the mile walk to the Edgar Allan Poe National Historic Site.

I do not often leave out details, Reader, but I did neglect to tell you about a certain waste of time in Richmond, Virginia. The Edgar Allan Poe Museum was a crummy little tourist trap with little useful information, a few sub-par exhibits, and a confusing map to follow through the tiny, disjointed rooms. To complete the scene, the snotty college flunky behind the desk easily snapped up our admission fees, with a barely grunted, "Hi". *The loser probably couldn't tell the difference between Annabel Lee and Lenore.* I only mention it to tell you not to go, and to contrast it with the Poe site in Philadelphia.

Though located outside of the main tourist square in downtown Philly, the EAP National Historic Site is run by park rangers who know their history. The building itself, not in the best neighborhood, but also not in the worst, is comprised of the stone house where Poe lived part of his adult life, as well as the adjoining house behind it. The downstairs has been (forgivably) converted into a cozy theatre where you can view a comprehensive biographical film on Poe, and a library where you can read or listen to one of the dozens of performances of Poe's works on cd. It crossed my mind that a bar or opium den might have been appropriate as well, but somehow I do not think the funding for it would pass.

Of course, the highlight for me was the upstairs, virtually untampered with since Poe's time. The small, cold, low-ceiling rooms served as bedrooms, each with fireplaces notched in the stone. It was in this home that Poe wrote his short story exploration of the guilty conscience, *A Tell Tale Heart*. Ba-boom. Ba-boom. Ba-boom. Though the stone floor had no floorboards, one could see how such a place would further develop his prose style. It was all so delightfully miserable! If I may degenerate into cliché, I was like a kid in a candy store… that only sold black licorice.

When my imagination finally had its fill, I dragged myself back downstairs and we browsed for a little longer before leaving. Senator seemed to enjoy the house, too, but with a more reserved appreciation than the big goofy grin on my face depicted. By the way, remember how I spoke highly of the guides in the museum? When they saw that we were about to leave in the rain, they offered to call us a cab. When we explained that we would be fine walking, they seemed genuinely concerned. Again with the brotherly love—I think I like Philadelphians.

We reached the car in the nick of time to make our escape. It was 3:00pm on a Friday afternoon in a major city, and the rain was picking up severely. If we did not get out of town then, we would probably still be stuck in traffic. It was a bit slow moving, but at least the route was clear and there was no construction. *What is this magical land?*

We had no other specifically planned stops, so the objective was simply to go west. We drove on, noting that the drenching gray somehow seemed to have washed the colors out from the trees over the past forty-eight hours. Suddenly things were looking like November. It was not boring, though. Battling the oncoming wind and hilly highways kept Senator in video game driving mode. I offered to drive, but he was a man on a mission, specifically that of the last leg of a road trip. He forged homeward, occasionally shuffling though radio stations for the latest rain report. Now and then a tunnel would offer a moment's reprieve, but almost as soon as we entered the mountain, we were returning out the other side to the downpour.

Eventually, around 9:00pm, the rain eroded our rock of determination into stopping for the night in West Virginia. This makes it sound like we took a wrong turn or some odd route, but there is actually an eleven mile wide strip of West Virginia that slices north between Ohio and Pennsylvania. If you ever had one of those puzzles where each state is a piece (except for the tiny New England states, which are always indignantly grouped together), it is the jutting part of West Virginia that always got smashed down, or chewed on, if there was a toddler in the house. Barely noticeable, this section of the state contains Wheeling, a fairly sizable town with all of your basic amenities and a casino to boot.

Thus, there we were, in the northern regions of Appalachia. Visions of fat men in overalls without shirts, playing jugs on porches vaguely crossed my mind. *I don't even know if I'm a Hatfield or a McCoy. Come to think of it, I rather fancied myself a Montague or a Capulet...* While it was true that we could barely understand the language, we found a clean, respectable chain hotel and checked in eagerly. In the brief walk from the car to the lobby, we were already wet enough to need dry clothes.

Once we accomplished that, the next order of business was food that did not involve us going out to get it. There would be no more propane picnics for the remainder of this trip. The only place that delivered was a pizza place, which made it an easy anonymous vote. Senator flipped on the Weather Channel, and I prepared to dance. I was hoping for some change in the forecast that would have meteorologists admitting they were wrong, consequently turning off the rain like a giant tap. Our wishes were not granted, but at least the pizza guy was knocking at the door. Growing up in Chicagoland, you never have unreal expectations regarding 'foreign' out-of-state pizza, but believe it or not, it was an aromatic, fresh, deep-dish pie. A few stupid cable shows later, we were asleep, anxious to get home the next day.

Saturday morning we woke up on our own, dressed in the most comfortable clothes that we had left, and checked out, pausing for a light breakfast in the hotel's lobby. More and more hotels are offering free continental[*] breakfasts, which are a nice touch if you want to drive as far as possible without stopping for lunch. We selected a few items and took a table next to three very excited middle-aged women. From what we could not help overhearing, they were on a ladies' weekend to the big city to go to the casino. They laughed and raised innocent heck as they downed their power breakfast, careful not to drop crumbs on their flashy casino wear. I tried to picture their massive frames balancing on stools in front of slot machines. Well, good luck to you all, I thought sincerely.

---

[*] I have no idea how this adjective can be applied to breakfast. One would assume that 'continental' refers to something of or concerning a continent. This appears to apply to pretty much any breakfast that is not being consumed on or over an ocean. Do ships and planes serve 'oceanic' breakfasts?

In the car we cranked the heat full blast, and rolled onto the entrance ramp with renewed purpose. In a few minutes we were out of West Virginia. Satisfied, I noted that we could cross yet another state off of our list. Ohio was generally uninteresting, but that is not always a bad thing when you want to get home. Senator continued to clip along into Indiana, and the clouds even started to break up.

A few times we had seen signs advertising Waffle House, a southeastern staple restaurant that had crept its way into the Yankee territory of Indiana. I remember seeing the signature block yellow signs when I was a kid, but never paid much attention to them. Senator was shocked at this revelation, and proclaimed his vision of us eating there. I agreed to keep my eyes open for the next Waffle House highway sign.

It was not long after that Senator got very dizzy suddenly. It was so bad that he pulled to the side of the interstate to switch places with me. Naturally I was concerned, but he said it was alright, and joked that he needed waffles to recover. When we passed the next WH sign, I ignored it, assuming he did not feel well enough to go, but I was immediately instructed to take the next exit.

Into Waffle House we strode. We were greeted by a waitress whose uniform unfortunately required her to wear an Aunt Jemima style cloth on her head. *Whose idea was this outfit?* I though it was a bit degrading, but she did not seem to mind. We gave our order, and were duly waffled. The maple pecan concoction was tasty, but the presence of three young children in the next booth hurried us along. Amazingly, Senator was soon feeling considerably better, too.

We were soon on the road, traversing the final stretch of land separating us from our home. The wind still pounded at us straight out of the west, but the rain had stopped completely. In one week's time we had toured a mansion, visited two sets of friends, explored historic sites from two wars, paid homage to the genius of Ben Franklin and Edgar Allan Poe, and touched the soil of eleven other states. Not too shabby for two kids and their faithful little pickup truck.

Chapter 5
The Paperback Writer Gets a Ticket to Ride: Early March 2007

I had not intended to return to Las Vegas, ever, really. We had gone there two years prior, and I had seen everything I wanted to, gambled a few dollars, and came back home, satisfied to check another one of America's landmarks off my list. Sometime in 2005, however, I learned of a new Vegas attraction that would warrant a few days back on The Strip. Cirque du Soleil, the French-Canadian born acrobat-theatre company, was adding another show to the roster. *Love* would be a tribute to the music of The Beatles. We might not have paid too much attention to this had it not been for two factors: 1.) we had already been awed by a Cirque show and knew they could deliver the goods, and 2.) George Martin, producer for The Beatles in the 1960s, was strongly consulted in the development of *Love*, with the full support of Paul, Ringo, and the families of John and George.

We were excited about this, as were Spencer and Michelle, our friends from New York. It was decided that we would meet in Vegas and go together. Conveniently and graciously, Spencer's parents had a home in Las Vegas, and they offered to let us stay there. It took over a year to set aside time, coordinate schedules, and get tickets, but by March 2007, we were on our way.

Now I am a girl who, while others curse with shovel in hand, can truly appreciate the beauty of winter. I enjoy the snow, and I do not even mind the crisp nip of cold air. Nevertheless, there is a significant difference between the crisp nip of cold air, and the violent, ravenous gnawing of arctic wind hovering in the negative double-digits. Now I know why Dante depicted the inhabitants of the deepest circle of Inferno encased in blocks of ice. February was downright painful throughout much of the Midwest, and by the time it was over, we welcomed any break. Yes, the southwest desert was sounding quite appealing as we packed and listened to the furnace kick in for the hundredth time that day.

Giddy with anticipation for the warm whirlwind weekend ahead, we set the alarm for 3:30am, and tried to get some sleep. As is often the case on a 'first vacation day', we woke up before the alarm and eagerly started our routines. From my post at the bathroom sink I could hear the joyous strains of *I Wanna Hold Your Hand* blasting from the other room. I smiled through the mad-dog foam of my toothpaste. Senator had officially kicked off the vacation. Could you imagine if every 4:00am were as fun and motivating as first vacation days? It would certainly improve workday attitudes.

We were loaded and on the road to O'Hare airport, driving through the wind-whipped snow. I did the standard mental check of anything imperative that I might have forgotten. All necessary items were aboard, but I made a startling discovery of another kind. Here we were, successfully on the road and technically on vacation, and there had been no hangups or disasters in the preceding weeks. This was momentous! Nothing had fallen apart, no cities were plagued, and there had been no tragedies. I am not superstitious, but even I was beginning to wonder. Now the perceived curse was finally broken, on our thirteenth trip, no less.* I smiled and informed Senator of our victory.

We arrived at the airport in plenty of time-- too early, in fact. Here I will open a general survey up to my readers: how early do you typically arrive at the airport before a domestic flight? For four years now we have religiously abided by the two hour rule, but I am starting to rethink this. Every time, we go through check-in and security, and then sit for an hour and a half. If we were to start going later, however, I am sure that would be the one time everything took longer.

On board the plane, we observed an unusual situation. Our pilot and co-pilot were females, and our cabin stewards were all male. While the women successfully proved that they could handle the aircraft smoothly, the men were having a little trouble on their end. I was parched, but both times up and down the aisle, the drink cart missed us. I tried the polite 'hey there' smile, but the boys did not notice me. Honestly, how do you skip a row of seats when you are going right down the aisle? And if you do miss them, don't you notice your error as you survey the rest of the happy passengers with their delightfully

---

* I have always argued that if there were such a thing as a lucky number, thirteen would be it, partly due to the fact that so many abhor it. But then again, my mother would tell me I was saying that just to be contrary. To her, I offer up this evidence: 1.) it was on the 13th that I was liberated from an evil ex, and 2.) my Essential Other was born on the 13th. If I really wanted to fake my way through a career in numerology, I might also point out that there are sometimes thirteen full moon days in a year, and if you can't get lucky under a full moon, well...

quenching beverages? *Wait a minute-- one of these things is not like the others. Why are those three people looking sad and thirsty, and where are their empty four-ounce plastic cups?* We did finally get their attention, and then there was no end of it. They were tripping over themselves to accommodate us. Aha! There is still some glamour left in air travel.

The flight progressed along pleasantly. Three hours later, the captain announced that we would be landing in about twenty minutes. At this time, the in-flight entertainment began. No, I do not mean the movie; I mean the nut behind us. In a loud and overdramatic voice, the woman beckoned the steward. "I am so *sorry* to bother you, but this *man* has been kicking my seat the entire flight. My doctor says I have whiplash. I can't be kicked!" She pointed behind her in a sweeping gesture. The steward looked back questioningly to the quiet man behind the upset passenger.

"I'm sorry, ma'am. I have a prosthetic leg. I was not trying to kick you," he replied calmly. Good, I thought. What a perfect response to shup this witch up. We listened for her shamed apology. How wrong we were. She would not quit.

"*Some* people need to spend the money for first class or extra leg room. I don't care. I will *not* be intimidated by him!" She was like some female assertiveness self-help course gone bad. *That's right, sister. Fight for truth, justice, and the ignorant way.* Again the astonished passenger behind her apologized. The steward rolled his eyes, and asked them to try to get along for the next fifteen minutes. I think he was suppressing the same comments we all were.

It seemed we were drama-free until she started up one last time after landing. She appealed to the trapped soul next to her, loud enough for six other rows to hear. "I mean *really*. He *obviously* needs to spend the money and sit somewhere where he can kick for the entire flight." Wow, is all I can say. I would advise that she exercise a bit more discretion in the future. In a hostage situation, she would surely be the first target... and I'm not sure her fellow travelers would throw themselves in harm's way to save her.

We arrived in Las Vegas to a smiling Michelle who greeted us and walked with us to meet Spencer. He was parking the convertible that his parents let us borrow. Flashing a birthday boy grin, he gave us the update on the plans for the weekend. He and Michelle were technically there on business (yeah, right), so we would have to swing by one of Michelle's client stores for a half hour or so. There we would also meet up with his parents for lunch. He then got down to the business of briefings. "Now my parents are very glad you are staying here, but they may talk your ear off. Also, my mom will try to feed you and give you advice. She's a typical Jewish mom." *So what was my Protestant mom's excuse*, I wondered. "When we go out to eat, they might complain about the service or the food." Michelle let out a sigh. "Other than that, it'll be fine." He smiled in annoyed assurance.

Our foursome nestled into the car and drove to the mall. That's right. You read me. The mall. Don't get too excited, though. I wasn't there to shop; it was just a convenient rendezvous point. Michelle was dispatched to meet her client store, and we were introduced to Spencer's parents, Bert and Carol of Las Vegas, by way of Long Island. They were marvelous. One talked over the other as they relearned our names and asked about our flight and suggested restaurants for lunch and refuted each others' suggestions (is that the place with the slow service or the other one?) and told us all about their evening's plans, and how it would be boring because their neighbor is nice but boring and they would probably be home by nine, much earlier than all of us, but enough about them. Spencer need not worry. We were already having fun with his parents, but I guess it is always different when it's your family.

To kill time while Michelle was in her meeting, our remaining five sauntered into the mall. Bert explained that the name Fashion Mall was due to the fact that there were often fashion shows right in the center of the mall. Sometimes concerts too. Enjoying the tour, I suddenly noticed that Spencer was no longer with us.

Shortly he rejoined us, proudly displaying his thumb. "Look! It's buffed!" Indeed, his thumbnail gleamed most unnaturally. The Israeli girl at the nail-buffing-machine kiosk had given him a free sample. He had even talked her into a second free buffing, feigning interest in the machine she was selling. I looked at my own dull nails. I'd make a terrible metrosexual. *Maybe I should experiment with the small belt sander when we get home.*

Soon enough Michelle joined us, equally disturbed and intrigued by the crystal gloss of her husband's thumbs. Together, we headed for Peppermill's, a funky, casual, and comfortable restaurant revered by the locals for its huge (or 'yewge', in the case of native New Yorkers) portions. We could order whatever we wanted, but someone at the table would be required to order the large fruit plate. "You won't even believe how big it is!" Bert extolled.

"I think I see one. There-- look at what's coming to those people. I told you it was yewge!" Carol confirmed Bert's statements on the produce volume. As we waited for our food, Bert began to entertain us with stories of the local political corruption. It was just like being back home in Chicago. My favorite tale was the one about the mayor, who, when responding to fourth graders' question of what he would take with him on a desert island answered, "A bottle of gin." One has to admire the rare quality of honesty in a politician.

When Bert began another story, Carol unintentionally took over until he cut in. "Hey, I thought I was telling this story," he reprimanded.

"Oh, that's right. Sorry. Go ahead." But he didn't. The moment was lost. The next instant none of it mattered anyway, because the LARGE FRUIT PLATE was making its entrance. It was everything we had always dreamed of for the last fifteen minutes, and more. Lettuce laid the soft foundation for the crown jewel, a carved pineapple filled with strawberries, watermelon, grapes, bananas, and citrus slices galore. The server lay the rainbow masterpiece gently at the center of the table. A misty hush fell over the booth. A few of us wept. Good call Bert and Carol.

Basking in the afterglow of the LFP, we followed our weekend adoptive parents back to their home. They gave us the tour and showed us the essentials. Their home is beautifully airy and tastefully decorated with unique objects and paintings from around the world, but the real treasure is the back porch. With an uninterrupted view of the mountains, it is not difficult to fall captive to a late afternoon desert siesta. And that is just what we did.

When the time came to pull ourselves up off the lounge chairs, it suddenly occurred to me that it was *Love* night. We would all see the show we had been talking about for a year and a half. Before that, though, we would enjoy dinner at the trendy new restaurant, Mix. I think the choice of restaurant was partly due to the fact that it fell into that sublime category of 'business expense' for Spencer. Whatever the reason, it was a night to celebrate. We waited in the lounge until our table was ready.

The lounge is definitely the highlight of Mix. From its vantage point high above The Strip, the view is unmatched. All of the spectacularly lit hotels and casinos are visible. The service however, left much to be desired.[*] We sat at a table in the uncrowded room for quite sometime, but no server came over. Hhmmm, shunned for drinks twice in one day. Maybe it's us.

---

[*] See, I fit right in with Spencer's parents.

Of course, as soon as Spencer went up to the bar, a server came by. The funny thing was that she initially skipped us for the next table, who had just been sat. When she finally did come to our table, we told her we had already ordered at the bar. She looked put out. I think she was glad when we left the lounge to be seated for dinner.

The dining room at Mix is something of a large white futuristic cavern with a yewge glass bubble sculpture raining down. We took our seats under Lawrence Welk's acid nightmare, and reviewed the menu. It was not my intention to slum it, but there were only two vegetarian options on the list, and Senator was ordering the other one. Besides, I actually was not very hungry. "I'll have the glorified macaroni and cheese[*], please."

Since we would not be back to the homestead for many hours, this was a good time to excuse myself to use the restroom. Those who know me know that I have a largely irrational fear of public washrooms. In short, I hate them. This was first discovered when I was two years old. A few hours into a road trip, my parents encouraged me to try to use the potty at one of the rest stops. I calmly informed them that I would wait until we got home... a week later. Public restrooms are merely chambers of germ-breeding strangers next to whom I cannot bring myself to tinkle, no matter how much coffee I've had. Through the years I've probably done irreparable damage to my kidneys, but I am working on this issue. Baby steps.

With this in mind, I pioneered the restroom. Then I remembered what kind of place I was in. Of course there would be an attendant. Of course I was the only customer. It's bad enough using the facilities, without someone monitoring me from just outside the door, patiently waiting with towel in hand to welcome me back. Here's a thought: how about I tip you to

---

[*]not actual name of dish

not assist me. After all, I have handled this process with relative success since I was two years old.

Making as little eye contact as possible, and thankful for the fact that the lady did not seem to speak English, I snaked my way out of the bathroom. Senator silently applauded my latest conquest. When the main course arrived, I tasted his dish, which involved truffles, and was tender and excellently seasoned. Mine was basically macaroni and cheese, with the distinction of a steak and lobster price tag. Now you know why I will never be a restaurant critic.

Who cares anyway? We were off to see *Love*. We drove to the Mirage hotel complex and waited in line at the theatre entrance. Beatles music played, the floor glowed rotating colored lights from underneath, and Sgt. Pepper-attired ushers herded the crowd inside. The theatre, built in the round, had surround sound speakers in every seat. Nice touch.

As with any Cirque du Soleil show, from the first note it was nonstop sensory overload. The four catwalks continually hosted Dr. Seusslike characters, dancing and twirling Beatley props. Above, ropes dropped down as acrobats spun and twisted. Often background screens played film footage from the 1950s and 60s. In the center 'ring' songs were dramatized in flipping, dancing, and a general outpouring of energy. All the while the music was pumping. Intermission, schmintermission. There was no breaking the momentum. Without giving too much away, I will tell you that you may find yourself temporarily under a giant sheet with a few thousand other people, covered in paper flower confetti.

All in all the show was amazing, but you would not want to be there if you do not like Beatles music. In truth, awesome though the experience was, we actually preferred the Cirque show *O*, to *Love*. The moral of the story, Reader, as preached in my last travelogue, is to pick out a Cirque show and delve into it. You will not be disappointed, whatever your taste.

Sunday morning we rose gradually, sipped our coffee, and related the details of *Love* to Mom and Pop. They were interested, but there was a more pressing issue on Carol's mind. What were our plans for dinner? Should she cook? Go out? If so, where?

We soon realized that the answers to these questions would require far more strategic tactics than those we typically employed. Opting to go out might suggest that we were expecting to be entertained, or worse, a free handout. On the other hand, staying in might suggest that we expected Carol to slave over a hot stove on our behalf. We weren't going anywhere near this one. We tried to leave the decision making up to Spencer and Michelle, who initially attempted the delay strategy, side-stepping any real answer. *C'Mon, guys. Even I can see through this one.* Eventually Spencer, well-versed in the game, presented the idea of appetizers at home and dinner out. Perfect. Everyone seemed generally happy, and by the time evening rolled around Carol was cooking us a large meal. We all knew better than to ask.

Besides the Cirque show, the other objective for this trip was to hike in Red Rock Canyon State Park. Located a half hour or so west of town, these gorgeous hills (or mountains, depending on your relative hometown geography), place marbled red and white rock against a cloudless desert sky. The four of us hiked for some time, then took a break, perched in a crevice some distance above the established trail. It was here, in the midst of small talk, that the concept of the Grudgekeeper was born.

I made a comment to the effect that I don't hold grudges. Senator immediately shot back with, "Oh, I do." It was funny for a second, and then it struck me. What if there was a service that held your grudges for you. We could sell the public on the idea of better health and more restful nights, all with the knowledge that somewhere, a faithful representative was still holding on to their anger and bitterness twenty-four hours a day. For a small fee you could rest assured that the jerk who wronged you would never be off the hook. We might even run sales. Buy two, get one free. First month is only a dollar. All grudges against family members half off during the holidays. The possibilities are endless, and if you steal this idea, Reader, there will be more than a grudge to haunt you.

With our future financial security in place, we wandered back to the trail. We left the park just in time to miss the bulk of the tourists*. Spencer, riding the crest of his birthday weekend, decided we must all experience the In-and-Out Burger. The name concerned me a little, causing me to ponder whether it referred to the speed of service, or simply the digestive process. Happily, it was the former. We nibbled our fries outside in the sunshine, preparing for the next gastronomic sin.

During our last visit to Las Vegas, we had discovered Freed's Bakery, the cake lovers' haven that sells wedding cake by the slice. Now we were anxious to share our frosted secret with our friends. Senator stepped to the counter and ordered a buffet of flavors, with four forks to sample. Again we found sunny seats to enjoy the decadence. I don't think our friends got as much out of it as we did, but they indulged our passions nonetheless.

It was on to the final stop of the day. We had gone to the Liberace Museum during our last stint in Las Vegas, and now our friends wanted to check it out. This would give us a chance to further explore the relation between Senator's family and the great, glittery Liberace. As the story goes, whenever Liberace would come on television, Senator's grandmother would point to the t.v. and announce, "That's your cousin!"

---

*Someday someone will point out to me that I am one of them, and I will pout.

The family would sort of nod appeasingly. "Sure, Grandma. That's great." Mainly there was disbelief, but enough curiosity that we decided to look into it further during our last trip to Vegas. When we viewed the biographical documents on the wall, there was a portrait of Liberace's beloved mother, with the same (maiden) surname as Senator. Also on display was a copy of the Ellis Island document of Liberace's maternal grandfather, also linking the family name with an established date of immigration that concurred with our records.

This trip we were able to effectively piece a bit more of the puzzle together, as our friends enthusiastically joined in our research, too. Eventually, we narrowed it down to two possibilities: either Senator's paternal grandfather was a brother, or a cousin to Liberace's mother. No, we were not counting on any inherited Rolls Royces, but it was fun performing amateur genealogy.

We trickled our way through the rest of the museum, past the outrageous sparkling and fabulously modified cars, and into the costume gallery. The sequins and rhinestones of the twenty or so stage costumes shined upon the room's centerpiece. There, on a pedestal, sat Liberace's famous mirrored piano, polished and tuned to perfection. We walked around it, commenting on the fuchsia boa and candelabrum that adorned it.

Finally, we ended our tour where all tours end, in the gift shop. Senator selected a souvenir to take back to his mom, and produced his credit card to pay for it. Hamming up his connection to the Big L, he said in a friendly voice to the cashier, "Look, I'm related!"

"Oh, do you play the piano?" She asked.

"Yes," he admitted, a little uncomfortably.

"Would you like to play his piano?" She casually offered.

"No!" Senator was stunned, responding in awed horror before he could even think. Thank goodness he had three good friends who mercilessly pounced on him during this once-in-a-lifetime moment.

"You *have* to!" I commanded, green eyes ablaze. We all started to talk over each other.

"You're never going to have this chance again!"

"You'll hate yourself later if you don't take this opportunity!"

"Do it for your mom!"

"Do it for Liberace!"

"Do it for yourself!"

"Do it because if you don't you'll never hear the end of it from us!"

As reality gradually set in, and he knew he had no choice but to go ahead and seize the day, Senator gave the cashier one final well-okay-if-you're-really-serious look. She immediately produced the proper waiver for him to sign. This was serious business. The next step was the ceremonial hand-washing. Okay, it was not exactly ceremonial, but the poor guy stepped out of the bathroom to the three of us hounding him with dumb grins on our faces.

The museum attendant then ushered him to the platform in the middle of the room. "This one?!" While we all understood the full extent of the museum's generous offer, Senator thought he would be playing some piano in a back room, alone. By now the onlookers had formed a small audience. I felt a little bad as one of the staff members invited us to take all the pictures we wanted, after she had just reprimanded a nice old man for snapping a single shot.

After a few seconds the shock wore off and Senator knew he was past the point of no return. Soon he was running his fingers over the keys beautifully. Though the boy will swear until he is a hundred years old that he "can't play", he must be one heck of a faker. It was amazing, and I wanted him to go on for hours. He only played a few minutes, and I think the whole episode was somewhat of a blur to him, but I was extremely proud. We took our specially-sanctioned photos and left the piano, chattering nonstop. Before we left, the cashier who started it all gave Senator a post card of The Piano, and told him that his name would be entered on a register of those who had played it. We have not seen the list, but we are told it is not long.

Man alive, as my dad used to say. This honor was the musical equivalent of a tour guide asking me if I wanted to write a chapter with Oscar Wilde's favorite pen. No, I think it was even cooler than that. And the icing on the cake: they never put the admission charge through on my credit card for our four tickets. Now that's class, baby.

Once you unexpectedly play the world-famous instrument of a international figure, the rest of the day is pretty anticlimactic, but it was enjoyable nonetheless. We rode our high back to Bert and Carol's home, where Spencer's mom was preparing multiple dishes for a 'simple buffet dinner', leaving savory smells to waft from the kitchen. No, I have no idea what happened to the appetizers in/dinner out plan, but this was preferable. While dinner finished cooking and we unwound, we visited and got the update on all kinds of people we do not know and will never meet. In fact, there is a very good chance that I know all about your personal and professional life, Reader, but don't worry; I won't tell.

Enjoying our delicious meal, somehow the dinner conversation evolved into the huge potential that the Grudgekeeper concept held. Already overtired, overexcited, and generally oversilly, we offered up the services of the Grudgekeeper. We had now officially opened Pandora's Box. "Oh, I got some grudges for you!" Bert laughed. The table suddenly overflowed with tales of slightings by family members, wrongdoings by acquaintances, and other fascinating historical data. At one point I was not quite sure if I was supposed to take it all seriously, but then, thankfully, the table erupted in laughter. Still, I have not shelved this Grudgekeeper thing...

Dinner and grudges finally wound down, and we cleared the table lazily. A distinct lack of motivation was engulfing us. So what do you do for entertainment in Las Vegas to conclude such a rampantly joyful day? First, you go change into your jammies. Next, you find a comfy seat on the couch, with plenty of pillows and good company around. Last, you push 'play' on the dvd player and watch as the music swells, the fireworks fly, and the announcer proclaims, "Jackie Gleason... The Honeymooners..." At least, that is what we would do.

Monday morning came all too quickly, and the weekend party was breaking up. Michelle had to fly back to New York, and Spencer had to attend to legitimate business, so we were dropped off on our own on The Strip. Armed with $20 in free slot machine credits, we decided to gamble, although, technically, I guess we were not risking anything, so I am not sure it counts as gambling. We played a few machines, and then switched to others. They were good for a half hour of laughs in between other conversation, but I do not know how people can do this for hours at a time. If Senator was not there, I would have been as bored as the Maytag repairman from the old commercials.

Of course, I cannot complain too much. I did win $3.34. I proudly stepped up to the cashier to claim my reward. I made the mistake of thinking I could joke with her as I plunked down my cash voucher. "I have to be able to say I came out ahead in Vegas," I kidded.

"Do you have ID?" she demanded accusingly, ignoring my well-meaning gesture. I produced. She scrutinized. "You don't look like you should be in here," she mumbled, shelling out the $3.34. I thanked her for the compliment, but I fought the urge to hang on Senator and tell the crabby cashier that I come here because their 'clients' pay the best.

We still had enough time for a classic buffet lunch, so we meandered toward one of the dining rooms of the casino. Buffets are getting out of control. It was a good thought to create separate food stations for crowd flow purposes, but now there are so many that you spend the entire time walking the perimeter of the room. Instead of tables for Asian or European fare, they have now evolved into full continents. *Baby, where'd you go? Oh, I think I see you in Mexico. Just let me grab my Thai spring roll and I'll meet you at our table in Australia.* At least you burn some of the calories this way.

We nibbled a few disappointingly bland desserts with our coffee and set out for a walk along The Strip. The sun was shining and we kept up a good pace, ignoring the occasional sideliners offering us free tickets. "...But this one doesn't have nude girls or anything..." the girl promised. I thought about telling her that's why I wasn't interested, just to see the look on her face. I guess I was in a feisty mood.

Time eventually expired and we took a cab to the airport. After walking the marathon from check-in to gate, we collapsed on the waiting area chairs. For tradition's sake, we bought a couple of cinnamon rolls, but sleep seemed far more appealing. Once aboard the plane, two sets of eyes began to droop contentedly. I was just about to slump down in my seat when I thought of one question. "So what song was that, that you played on Liberace's piano?"

"Key of D."

Chapter 6
Then Maybe One Day: Late April 2007

After a few last nods to winter, northern Illinois began to melt into spring. Consequently, we made our annual plans to upgrade the yard with new foliage. Sometime early in April we placed an order for a few dozen bushes, fifty bulbs, and scores of lavender starters. Assuming that it would not be shipped until May, as was the case the previous year, we put the outdoors on the back burner of our minds, and focused on the upcoming trip to-- you guessed it-- New York City.

New York is, to me, the hometown that I never lived in. And, to be completely truthful, maybe I would not even like living there permanently. Nevertheless, my affair with this micro-America has been going strong for years now, and I actually get a touch of homesickness if I go too long without visiting New York.* Imagine my delight, then, when on New

---

*Senator now jokingly asks me if it's 'safe' before putting on a Woody Allen movie. Translation: If we spend the next two hours watching this, are you going to spend the next two months whining about going to New York?

Year's Day, while ordering plane tickets for the Las Vegas trip, I *accidentally* found round trip tickets to New York for just $92 per person. We could not drive there for that cheap! Thus, the tickets were ordered, another vacation was planned, and you now have to sit through yet another chapter on the Big Apple. My apologies.

    April flew by and soon it was just one week until we were scheduled to leave. This is always a mildly tense time for us, given our track record for pre-vacation disasters, but the curse seemed to have been broken last time, so we were optimistic. Friday afternoon I leaned out of the front door to check the mail. *Oh crap!* It wasn't bad news, exactly. It was just that, there on the front deck lay the infamous green shipping bags containing over 100 plants in need of finding good homes in our yard. The leafy orphans had arrived several weeks early, coinciding with a sudden cold, rainy spell in the weather, and busy work schedules that left us no extra time prior to the trip.

    It was begrudgingly decided that Senator would take a day off and I would join him after working a half day. We would then commence the great Spontaneously Mandatory Arbor Day at our house. The night before, the weather forecast predicted temperatures in the 40s, with ambient sleet. This was not going to be the pastoral, romantic tilling of the homestead that I had imagined. I dozed off planning how many layers of clothing I would need to work outside all day.

    As it turned out, the mercury soared into the low 60s, it never sleeted, and almost all of the plants survived their fevered installation. Of course, there was that one point when I stooped to enlisting the help of the four year old boy next door when I needed to clear out some weeds. In my defense, it gave his parents a break, and he was quite proud that I needed him. I did not even feel ashamed when I accepted his offer to use his little plastic wheelbarrow. All in all, it was a satisfying challenge well met, and we could finally turn our brains back to our trip.

When your flight leaves at six-whatever in the morning, and you have to leave your house at three-whatever, everything takes on a dreamlike state. We parked the car and rode the shuttle to the terminal. "What airline?" the driver asked.

"Yes."

"Uh, ATA," Senator expounded upon my reply. Getting off the bus, I staggered toward the terminal doors, almost forgetting my travel documents on the seat. Bleary eyed, I propped myself against Senator and tried to stay awake through the check-in line. Security was not open yet, so we descended to the only available drink stand.

I thought an orange juice might help my composition, so I chose one and began to dig out my money. The morning counter girl was still stocking the cooler, and as revenge for making her work so early, distinctly sold me a warm juice, instead of the one I had chosen. Boooo. *Oh well. Something cold might have been too much of a shock to my system anyhow.*

We selected a few vacant seats within earshot of the janitors. They were all worked up about some recent labor issue that currently evades my memory. The leader was stirring the others up. At any moment I expected one of them to yell a hearty, "Amen!" So if you are a manager concerned about union organizers, you might want to check out what they are doing and to whom they are preaching at four in the morning.

Before we could lend our solidarity, the security lines opened and it was time to move along. I muddled through another checkpoint, almost falling over as I took my shoes off to pass through the detectors. It struck me that it would be funnier if, instead of the guards periodically yelling into the crowd that travelers had to take their shoes off, there was a giant sign that read: REMOVE THY SHOES, FOR THOU ART STANDING ON HOLY GROUND. Alas, I suppose Judeo-Christian reference humor has no place in the public airport.

Finding seats in our gate area, I once again began to fade from consciousness, nestled between my sweatshirt and Senator's arm. It was warm, so warm, and I was dreaming that I was in my own bed, floating, floating, until--

"Flight 422 nonstop to La Guardia now boarding all rows." Up we rose and lined up one last time for the ramp. Except, there was no ramp. It felt like we were on candid camera as our group was sent through an unmarked door, down some very industrial-looking stairs, and right out some obscure portal. The attendants said the ramp was broke, so we had to use the stairs to the plane, a la 1964 Beatles. We could have had fun with that if we weren't so tired.

We crawled into our economy seats and tried to go back to sleep. They say that when you shut out one of your senses, the others are intensified. This is true. When I close my eyes, I can hear more distinctly. The only problem is that I hear stupid conversations more distinctly as well. The large woman behind me began to orate in fluent Ebonics. "What is dat? A kid. No! It's a cat! Dat lady has a cat wid her! Can't nobody be bringin' no animals wid 'em. I cannot believe dat! What if I is allergic or somethin'. Can't be havin' no damn cats wid you on no plane." She beckoned the flight attendant for confirmation. "Miss, Miss. Can she have her pet wid her?" She gestured to the woman a few rows back.

"Yes, Ma'am. She bought a seat for it."

"What?! When did ya'll start dat?"

"We've done it for at least the twenty years I've worked here."

"Shhh... Well what udder airline do not let people bring dey animals?"

"I'm pretty sure they all do, Ma'am. Was there anything else I can help you with?"

Don't get me wrong. It didn't break my heart that I was not sitting by the cat lady, but I also know when to keep my

mouth shut (usually). So phone in your votes for biggest plane crab now. Press *1 to vote for the Las Vegas "he-won't-stop-kicking-me-with-his-prosthetic-leg" lady. Press *2 to select the New York "I-can't-believe-dey-can-bring-dey-pets" lady.
E-mail me for results.

    The flight was ideally pleasant, and I was even able to nod off a few times. About a half-hour outside of New York, I conveniently got a second wind. Suddenly I was excited. Soon the familiar landmarks came into view, and once again it was real. My renewed energy kept me alert as we rounded the harbor and crossed the Brooklyn Bridge.

    Wow, we're really banking hard. We had made this same trip several times and I never recalled it being so tight. The runway seemed to zoom toward us from the side. From my window seat over the port side wing I could see that we were entirely too close to the runway to still be angled so strongly. For the first time, I was terrified of a landing. The wing looked like it would scrape the ground violently at any second, and I braced myself. *No, wait-- maybe we should go limp.* At the last possible second, and I do not say this for the sake of drama, the plane jerked level, and started to brake like we were careening to the edge of the earth. Carry-on bags flew forward from the grasp of unsuspecting passengers, as we all let out relieved breaths. I looked over at Senator as I handed other peoples' escaped belongings over the back of my seat. *What the heck was that all about?!* At any rate, we were definitely awake now.

    Anxious to get to our friends' home, we collected our suitcase as quickly as possible and grabbed a cab. The stress of the crazy landing made the bathroom my primary goal, which was not aided by the fact that the rotten cabby took the longest possible route to lower Manhattan. *Tip, schmip, my good man.* We got out and walked the last two blocks, passing the armed guards of the Federal Reserve Building. This is always a somewhat eerie site, which is reason enough to be grateful for the country in which we live. I pray we never live to see the day when riflemen on street corners do not catch our attention as extraordinary.

Ah! The familiar tower. Spencer and Michelle were still working, so we let ourselves into their apartment. The dogs went wild. "They're back! They're back! They came back to play with us! Let's go for a walk! How 'bout the park! Did you see my new water dish? If you'll just get our leashes we could show you two kids around town..." I patted my way past them and into the bathroom.

Ah! The familiar non-public restroom. I completed my business, checked the mirror to assess how frazzled I looked, and turned to leave. *Wait a minute. Why is the floor wet?* The toilet was not overflowing, and I was pretty sure I had not missed. Then I realized the pipes were leaking. Now this is not the circumstance with which one wishes to introduce one's presence as a guest. Fortunately, I could defer to my more-householdly-adept half. "Senator!..." Unfortunately, there was nothing he could do either. We sopped up the little puddle and resolved to use the other bathroom whenever possible.

To the acute disappointment of two aged dogs who did their best poor-abandoned-puppy impressions, we left for the street. Remembering a great little juice bar a block away, we followed the sweet smell of ripe fruit inside. Feeling invigorated, and inspired by the latest health book that I had read, I opted to add wheat grass to my drink. If you are not familiar with wheat grass, it can best be described as its name implies, except for the wheat part. Its detoxifying effects on the body's many systems are celebrated by cultures worldwide, but to look at it, you would think you were about to ingest a Chia Pet. Senator glanced at me in awed surprise. "Do you know what you're getting into?" I played it cool.

The juice jockey behind the counter then caught me off guard. "Inside or shot?" he asked.

"Uhhh..."

"He means the wheat grass," Senator subtly informed, "You probably want it mixed in your drink."

Though I truly wanted to go hardcore, the thought of puking my toxins out down Broadway was not appealing. "Inside is fine."

Apparently the Grassmaster had me pegged flatteringly wrongly, thinking I would choose the shot. The cup was already full and he had not yet added the green fairie. This perplexed him. I assumed he would either dump some out, or put it in a bigger glass, but instead I was commanded to, "Drink some." I chugged away, now on the spot and holding up the line. Like a trick glass, nothing seemed to disappear. "Drink some more." *Yes, Grassmaster.* When the sufficient vacancy was created, he added the wheat grass and sent us on our way. I felt as though I had passed some initiation test to determine my grass-worthiness. Now a member of the club, I happily nursed the rest of the drink, with only a minor passing sense of nauseous doom. As for Senator, the boy slammed a straight shot of wheat grass juice in a split second. *Show-off.*

We meandered around until we found ourselves in Chinatown, home of the $2 knock-off souvenir. Occasionally, great treasures are to be found here. A shelf full of folding fans in one shop caught my fancy. At that time, my sister was decorating her new apartment in reds and blacks, and I thought a Chinese red embroidered fan would be a perfect homewarming accent. I chose one, but the stitching was loose and falling apart. When I picked up the second one, I realized it was pink, not red. Carefully, I put those back and began the quest for the right fan.

It was not long before the dragon store owner accosted me. "Aw da same! Onee needa open waaaan!" she reprimanded. I tried to explain that some were not made as well as others, while casually drawing her attention to the fact that everything I rejected was placed gently in its proper spot. "No-- aw da same!"

Indeed they were not all the same, but by this time she had far invaded my personal space, so I decided it was time to leave. The upside to such a situation in Chinatown is that, perhaps more so than anywhere else, you really can say, "I don't need your crummy junk! I'll take my business right down the road/next door/across the street/behind the alley!" I have yet to figure out how fifty shops selling the same products can compete, unless they are all part of an Asian conglomerate that will take over the New York economy.

We wandered some more, and ended up back at our friends' home, but not before buying a bag of roasted mixed nuts for the walk. The dogs greeted us anew. "Great! You're back! We knew you didn't forget about us! Now here's what we were thinking..." Thankfully, the toilet pipe had not dripped anymore since we had left, so we sprawled on the couch for a nap. This time I was out cold. No gentle dozing here. When I awoke, almost three hours later, I did not know where I was for a second or two. *Hhmmm. Street sounds below. Large building next door. Ah, yes-- now I remember.*

Soon Spencer and Michelle came home, and the dogs presented us, asking if they could keep us. The evening's plans included dinner at a new, casually trendy Chinese restaurant. "Speaking of Chinese, Wendy got us kicked out of a Chinatown store during our first hour in New York," Senator quipped.

"I did *not* get us kicked out; I simply chose to patronize other comparable establishments due to a difference in opinions on the quality inspection rights of customers regarding potential product purchases," I retorted.

"You got us kicked out, Baby."

This time I couldn't keep a straight face. "Onee needa open waaan!" I did my best angry shopkeeper impression for our friends.

Rallying the dogs for a 'business walk', we stopped by the local coffee/wine bar to claim the free bottle of wine that our friends had won previously. One of the touches I adore about New York City is the class that even the smallest establishments can exude. The café was half the size of our house, but that did not stop the twenty-something behind the counter from formally presenting the free bottle to our table, complete with candlelight and assortment of gourmet cheeses. Very nice.

When we had finished our appetizer, we walked the dogs back home and piled into The Car. During the previous year our friends had purchased a car. This is a major decision and commitment for a New Yorker, where fewer than 20% of the population are auto owners. The purchase is easy; the parking can be a nightmare.

Between Spencer and Michelle, they had a system worked out, and they were getting pretty darn good at it. On Friday nights he drove the car home, stealing a parking spot in their Financial District neighborhood, which promptly kicked the suits out at five o'clock. Over the weekend it wasn't too bad, provided they were moved out of the spot early Monday morning. During the weekdays, the car could be kept in a garage further away. There was definitely a science to the whole matter, and more than once it involved Michelle physically guarding a vacant spot while Spencer circled the block one more time before power parking. The cruel irony is that, once you get a good spot, you are almost willing to forgo the convenience of driving just to keep it.

Spencer chauffeured us to the restaurant, and after several failed attempts to find an empty spot, instructed us to get out and get a table. Okay. We stepped into the hopping restaurant and were promptly seated. As the server brought water and menus we explained that there would be four of us. "My husband's just parking the car," Michelle added.

"Oh," nodded the server understandingly, making a mental note that there would be no hurry to get back to our table. After what must have been fifteen or twenty minutes Spencer bounded through the restaurant entrance, victorious and beaming. Now we were ready to eat. In the past few years I have been exploring different Asian cuisines, and the many fresh vegetarian dishes on the menu sounded delicious. I did the sneak-peek at other people's plates as servers rushed by with hot meals. The savory smells were wonderful, and I made my choice.

In addition to the entrees, Senator was tempted into trying an appetizer involving hot peppers. Spencer, still riding high from his parking conquest, was up for the challenge as well. In normal culinary conversation, a 'hot' pepper might be a jalapeño, or, warmer still, an habeñero. Senator can easily down either of these, usually without the slightest grimace, but no so with the Chinese fire veggies.

He ceremoniously snapped apart his chopsticks and fished up a strand of pepper, popping it into his mouth. Instantly his eyes teared up. I then watched him evolve through a few different shades of red. He looked like he wanted to laugh, but he didn't dare open his mouth to add oxygen to the raging fire. Not to be outdone, Spencer also partook. Their strained silence left Michelle and me plenty of time to make fun of the situation. Not only wouldn't we try the peppers, but I was not sure if I could even take the heat of kissing Senator afterward.

Once the appetizers were survived by the males of the clan, our entrees came. Though I try to live the 'when in Rome' creed when in restaurants, I would like to know how exactly one eats a liquid based dish with chopsticks. I clumsily used mine to grab the big chunks of herbs and vegetables. My mind flashed to the two-year-old whom I often babysat, who now seemed like an expert with utensils by comparison. I wasn't sure whether to be grateful or embarrassed when the savvy waitress slipped me a fork and spoon. *No wonder you people stay so thin. Only a third of the food every makes it into the mouth.*

As it turns out, it is possible to get stuffed from light Chinese food. We proved it. Still, that did not stop us from accepting Michelle's offer to get cupcakes to bring home for a late dessert. She explained that she had stumbled across a local bakery that sold the World's Greatest Cupcakes, in her opinion at least. As we perused the display case, the choices looked promising: pistachio, red velvet, creamy vanilla. When we had each contributed to the final decision, we headed back to The Car, congratulated Spencer once more on a job well done, and drove home. As in Las Vegas, it seemed like closing the night out with a few episodes of The Honeymooners was the appropriate thing to do. This time, however, we were watching it in its proper setting. Somehow Ralph Kramden's big mouth was even more effective when you were within walking distance of Brooklyn.

Saturday would build on the Brooklyn theme, but first it was time for the ritual dog walking/coffee acquiring. Under a blinding sun we hiked along the East River up to the latest addition to the ever-growing chain of fun, hole-in-the-wall coffee spots. This was yet another tiny, tastefully cozy retreat that boasted no more than five or six tables. We squeezed our way inside and ordered.

It was here that I witnessed one of my all time favorite signs. Posted at the counter was the handmade commandment: No Cell Phones at Counter! Amen and thank you. If you have ever worked retail, or have ever been in a cashier's line behind someone yakking away on their wireless appendage, you can appreciate this. Phones and convenience, fine. Phones and convenience that do not obstruct basic manners, even better. That's me-- Emily Post for a new generation. Now if you'll excuse me, I must go polish the good silver in case guests come calling.

Armed with my coffee and the knowledge that civilization still exists in the Twenty-first Century, I joined the others on the bench outside. Strangers stopped to chat or pat the dogs, which became almost necessary if they wanted to pass by the sprawling relaxed beasts. It was beautiful out, but the sunshine had turned to glare, and, stupidly I had left my sunglasses at the house. Always resourceful, I realized that I was packing an ever-versatile banana, on behalf of my fruitophile boyfriend. I placed it over my eyes, and lay my head back on the top of the bench. My sleek shades had officially morphed me into a synthetic 1983 Carmen Miranda. I'm sure this drew a few stares, but what did I care? I could not see them.

After depositing the dogs at home, we once again piled into The Car. This time we were making the big leap, all the way over to Brooklyn. Our friends were planning to move there following the renovation of a penthouse apartment. The new 'hood was in transition, with elements of a rooted Polish community, a young single set, new business developers, and local musicians and artists.

In keeping with this atmosphere, we lunched at a small Polish restaurant, that had very few Polish items on the menu. The servers were... Polish mamas? Not even close. The place was staffed by pleasant, trendy post-punk kids. Again though, it was representative of the neighborhood, and most importantly of all, comfortable.

Next it was time to break-and-enter, which our friends euphemistically dubbed 'going to see our new pad'. Stealthily, we climbed the stairs through the crumbling halls that patiently awaited their turn at restoration. The crowning apartment and the roof deck of the seven-story building overlooked the river, a few of the landmark bridges, and even the Statue of Liberty in the distance, yet the surrounding streets were remarkably quiet.

We stayed just long enough to trace out imaginary walls and snap a few pictures. More ports of exploration loomed below.

As we walked toward the neighborhood's main streets, Spencer noticed some men in the open downstairs of another building that was getting rehabbed. Excited about new restaurants and shops moving into the area, and always up to meet a new local face, he stopped and asked what was going in there. Almost before he could finish the short sentence, the leader pushed his hand up in defense against us and curtly replied, "We're in a meeting."

Well alrighty then. Apparently the conservatively attired businessman was not the public relations representative. Potential responses might have included, "A new restaurant. You guys should stop in when it's finished," or "A gift shop. You guys live around here?" We quickly moved along. *I bet that guy uses his cell phone at the counter.*

We crossed the street to find a busy miniature downtown, complete with record stores, clothing shops, a flea market, and even a cheese shop. In my younger days I would have been prejudiced against such a place, preferring to remain loyal to Murray's. This, however, was the beginning of a new era. I warmed up to the Bedford Cheese Shop fairly quickly, aided by the free sample of a sharp aged formaggio from somewheria. The fact that Murray's had metastasized into a large store from the original cramped, nostalgic counter also put another boccacini checker on the Bedford side of the scales. Yeah, I was going to be alright with this. Sorry, Murray, wherever you are.

Our group collectively decided that we deserved naps, so back we drove, nabbing an impressively close parking spot. The vacancy, less than a block from the entrance of Spencer and Michelle's building, was a rare, legal find that had somehow evaded the notice of others. We were immediately blindfolded and sworn to secrecy. The person who would give away someone's secret parking spot, even under torture, was the lowest form of dirty traitor scum. In fact, several revisionist historians are exploring the plausible theory that Benedict Arnold's first act of betrayal was to reveal to the British Washington's favorite spot, not moments after he unhitched his horse.

We all marched inside. Soon four bodies were flung over various couches and chairs until the alarm went off. Snoozes interrupted, Spencer and Michelle dressed for the social obligation of a coworker wedding, but we had no such adult restraints. Saturday night in New York City was ours, though you may find this a letdown, Reader. The adventure was resoundingly mellow.

We browsed the local listings, but no concerts or plays caught our attention, so we decided to wander some main streets and catch a subway north until we felt like resurfacing for action. When we stepped outside, we found the spring breeze warm and exhilarating. We trekked the few minutes to the first available train station, but it was too nice to travel mole-style, so we agreed to remain on foot until the night became cold. Five hours later we found ourselves taking the last steps of our 'little walk'.

We never did hop a sub. We never stumbled across a musical venue of interest. We did not go to any tourist sites. Instead, we joined thousands of others, out doing what people do when they have no real plans. We watched the skateboarders in the park. We (literally) stopped and smelled the flowers lining the doorways of the mom-and-pop grocers, without buying a single one. We made fun of tourists paying So-Ho prices for clothing styles I could find at a decent thrift store. We peeked inside new trendy restaurants to admire or critique the décor. (Glass baubles seem to be in.)

As a fitting climax to the evening, we inadvertently ended up eating inside a kitschy middle-Americana diner. The primary-colored restaurant was painted with cartoon and pop figures from the last century. On each table was an inviting deck of Trivial Pursuit cards to pass the wait. Can you name the three European countries that begin with the letter A?[*]

Next question: what was the signature dish of this bistro? That would be tater tots. I chuckled to myself when I heard the woman in the booth behind us ask the server what a tater tot was. "Well, it's like a little fried potato ball," she described as best she could. The customer ordered some, probably thinking she was about to indulge in an improved version of a latke. Poor, unsuspecting native New Yorker, about to be taken on a culinary trip down memory lane to a school cafeteria in the Midwest.

Actually, there were many vegetarian options on the menu, and the ingredients were extremely fresh and well-seasoned. Though I have never liked tomato soup, I was inexplicably drawn to the tomato-cheddar soup, which quickly took the prize as the best soup I have ever tasted. *Fresh basil! Who saw this coming?* We completed our meal, gave a few more incorrect Trivial Pursuit answers, and walked the two miles back to our friends' home. Only once did we break pace to yield the right of way to a small rat. What an ironically perfect evening.

Despite the easygoing Saturday night, I woke up with a headache the next morning. I prescribed myself some fresh air and, how convenient, a vacation. Lazily we got ready to go out to breakfast with Spencer and Michelle at The Gray Dog Cafe, a popular morning haunt. The GDC, despite its ever-growing acclaim, left me with a love-hate opinion. On the one hand, it is a warm, visually ambient cafe, in a lovely old storefront. The coffee is quite good, too, which never hurts.

On the other hand, you should not bother going there unless you are alone. The room is small, but from the moment you step inside, the noise level is deafening. Then you order fast-food style, after waiting in a long, crammed line along the

---

[*]Albania, Andorra, Austria

counter, which is not conducive to visiting. When you are through ordering, you clumsily squeeze past other customers and staff with your silverware and coffee and hope for a table. If you find one, you then begin your shouting match. "WHAT ARE YOU GOING TO GET? I'M BETTING ON NOTHIN' AND SHAVING MY LEGS."

"WHAT?!"

"I SAID 'I'M GETTING A MUFFIN AND SHARING MY EGGS'." You can see the potential difficulties in normal conversation. The whole situation made me antsy to take my headache elsewhere, despite the excellent nothin' and legs.

Our next venture was far more soothing. The dogs once more took us for a walk. Battery Park has become one of my favorite New York-in-the-morning locations. The breeze off the water is refreshing, and it is prime people-watching territory. There are a few key players you can always depend on. First, you are guaranteed a long line of tourists, both domestic and international, waiting to board the ferry to Ellis Island. Some are simply curious, but others are on missions of personal genealogical significance. Second, there is always a jazz musician (or two or three, depending on how well the tips are flowing) in the park. The groove of the saxophone is a fitting soundtrack for a lazy Sunday morning here.

Finally, Battery Park hosts my favorite characters, the Statues of Liberty. 'Statues', plural? Indeed. These are fine souls who don their emerald robes and spiky foam crowns, scoping the area for tourists who would like to pose with them. (The better statues have light-up torches, if you are in the market for such a model.) I would love to see this job on a professional resume. Position: Statue of Liberty. Location: New York City, well, okay, actually Jersey, but don't tell anyone. Duties: greeting immigrants, symbolizing freedom, keeping traditional ties to the French, serving as a glorified lighthouse, inspiring a patriotic and profitable line of merchandise. Supervisors:

Washington Monument, Mount Rushmore. Don't forget your cameras, kids!

It was also among the magnificent background of New York Harbor that we first learned that our friend had once composed a song about a nearby municipal project. The city had begun digging a subway from the park, inspiring the aptly titled tune, *Diggin' a Subway* by our own Spencer. The compelling lyrics follow:

> Diggin' a SUB-way
> Diggin' a sub-WAY
> Then maybe one day
> We'll take that subway
> To Staten Island
> Terminal

Oh, how I wish I could sing the melody for you now, Reader, so that you too could experience the phenomenon of awakening with this catchy ditty in your brain, and finding yourself humming it in the shower, and musing whether it would be possible to tap out a recognizable version of it on the phone's keypad while on hold. It is evermore etched upon our minds and hearts as the theme song for Manhattan.

Performing various renditions of *Diggin'*, we ambled into the Stone Street area, a hidden gem of colonial inns, taverns, and shops, restored and recycled into new eateries and stores. The narrow cobblestone streets weave around this tiny district, providing a glimpse into New York's early days. Like everywhere else, development is moving in, but for the most part, it is being done with respect to the historical architecture. Hopefully it will retain its integrity amidst the asphalt jungle.

Alright, enough about the beauty of the city. It may have taken two books and fourteen chapters, but be satisfied to know, Reader, that we are human and have now experienced the Vacation Fight. *Damn. I thought we were above this.* Like all good rows, I do not recall the exact source of the conversation, but it somehow evolved into one of those sitcom classic moments where unexpected information about your loved one is revealed, via an innocent comment from a friend.

I will not go into details, mainly because it is nothing dramatic-- no affairs, long lost children, illegal activity, or secret rock-star tours. Nonetheless, said fact temporarily stunned me as I am used to comfortably talking about everything with Senator. I had to decide what to do. I swallowed my shock and stayed silent, determined not to make a scene. I was hurt, and I did not particularly want to be around anyone, but this was vacation, I was glad to be here, and I did not want to ruin it. I walked along with the other three, trying to focus on anything else until I could talk to Senator alone.

Here is where the paradox shines. Senator, generally a quieter personality than me, is, ironically, far more prone than I to reveal his true feelings in public, regardless of the circumstances. This is appreciated in cases like giving compliments, holding hands, or telling off a jerk, but not so good during Vacation Fight. In fact, his approach was the exact opposite of mine. In mid-stride, he stopped, announced to our friends and everyone on the street that there was a problem, and we were going to deal with it right now, or go home. I do not ever remember being so mortifyingly embarrassed. Fortunately, most of those around were non-English speaking Japanese tourists, but even they were temporarily deterred from their worship of the New York Stock Exchange to provide a captivated audience. *At least they are not taking pictures...yet.*

Thus, it had begun. Our friends, to their eternal credit, played it cool and suggested we meet back at their home later on. I briefly wondered if they were going home to toss our suitcases out the door. Well, when you are in the middle of a busy street and your boyfriend shows no sign of pursuing a quiet, reserved discussion, all you can do is choose some vacant steps to sit on together and let your guts and your emotions and your snot flow until some progress is made.

An hour later things weren't perfect, but they were much better. Next we had to handle problem number two: the awkward reentry into our friends' home. I could not stand much more humiliation in one day, so I rehearsed a few possible greetings in my head. There was the apology: *I am so sorry about all of this. Please forgive us and we won't cause any more problems.* I could also go for the vindictive approach: *I'm sorry my boyfriend felt the need to make a scene.* Most appealing, though, was the flat-out denial: *Hey guys! What's up? Any plans for tonight?* In the end we settled on a quick 'sorry' and 'thanks', and then the matter was dropped. Spencer and Michelle have now earned the Awesome Hosts Award for grace and excellence above and beyond the call of duty in creating a hospitable atmosphere and diffusing potential awkwardness.

We relaxed with snacks and walked to another park to watch the boats. It was the first good-weather weekend of the season, and hundreds of people were taking advantage of it. Picnickers filled their tummies and napped, while children played lawn games. Old timers traded stories and laughs, content to be the supervising generation. Best of all, not one of these people had witnessed our afternoon misery. It was like a giant oxygen mask; I inhaled deeply. This was good. I cleared my mind and my throat and began, *"Diggin' a subway..."*

The trip had silently been deemed salvageable, so we turned our thoughts to food (of course). Though the sunset had left the temperature considerably cooler, the idea of the season's first outdoor meal was very appealing. We hiked the few blocks back to Stone Street to an Italian restaurant. Inside, servers darted around the candlelit room, appeasing the warm crowd. Outside, we were joined by a few other stubborn tables who refused to admit it had become quite chilly. I am not complaining, though. The pizza and conversation were good, and the weather offered the ideal excuse to nestle in closely while we ate.

When the time came to leave, Senator once again took my hand as we walked a lethargic, overstuffed walk. My friend used to jokingly refer to relationship arguments as 'growing'. Then again, nothing grows faster than a weed, so what does that say? By that illustration, I guess we had sprouted an inch or two that afternoon, but things were generally settled, and we were in no hurry for any more growth spurts.

Just like the rest of the world, our Monday morning came much too soon. We bid an early adieu to our friends, who left for work. I give credit to anyone who showed up for work that day, as it was sunny, breezy, dry, and consistently in the mid-70s. The only clouds in the sky were the kind that exist solely for entertainment of the imagination. *Do kids still do that, or is it just me?*

We had no agenda, and Senator's only firm destination was the coffee shop. Left up to me, where else would we end up but in a graveyard? No trip to lower Manhattan is complete without at least passing Trinity Church on Broadway. The church dates back to colonial times, with an adjacent graveyard with the dates to prove it.

Reclined on the bench in the graveyard we were surrounded by dozens of beds of well-fertilized tulips. Our unnecessarily hot coffees steamed wildly. Conversation came slowly, interrupted by the occasional unusual tombstone that caught my eye. Strangely, the time in New York had gone by quickly, yet I felt that we had gone on a much longer trip. Ironically, I find that I get reflective about life when seated among the dead. It is short, too short for stress, and far too short not to enjoy every moment with my Essential Other. I inhaled my java, satisfied.

As we sat, the occasional group of tourists wandered around. An overweight senior citizen foursome with the giggles walked past, asking us to take their picture. As they posed and Senator took his stance with their camera, the ringleader gave orders. "I think we should stand like this. Now you move back further, young man. Make sure we all get in the shot." She would have been annoying if she wasn't so funny. I tried to imagine Spencer, Michelle, Senator, and myself in their roles, frolicking around New York in loud clothes. I can't wait...

In between the tourists, a few school groups toured the grounds. I failed to see how it was appropriate for the kindergarten class that marched by, but whatever. *Come to think of it, how come I didn't get to go to any graveyards in kindergarten? Zoo schmoo.* Then they really caught my eye. The teacher held the massive church door open and they filed in.

"You can go in there?!" I need say no more. Senator was already standing up and leading me toward the door. I had no idea that lowly outsiders like myself were welcome inside. For the first time in my life I was glad to be around a school group.

Trinity Church is just as impressive on the inside as it is on the outside. Dark, carved wood is abundant, and the English influence is apparent. Rows of hard pews keep the faithful awake. Lining some of the edges of the sanctuary are various religious icons and cenotaphs. Grandest of all is the altar, with massive stained glass windows rising in gothic arches above the crucifix centerpiece. Beneath Christ on the cross are his mother and closest disciples. This is truly one of America's most beautiful houses of worship. If you visit Manhattan and miss out on this, don't blame me; I told you.

There were only a few more hours to kill until we had to return to La Guardia. We took a final walk up Broadway, nabbing the favored treat of the neighborhood-- roasted, sugar-coated nuts. We turned down a random street to find a typical New York surprise. The plans for the small building site were scrapped when, upon digging for a new structure, the remains of several Africans were found. The burial ground is now marked and preserved as a National Monument, right in the middle of the city.

Our last stop before returning to the apartment to pack up was a nearby florist to purchase some 'thank you' flora. The flower vendors on the street are something I miss when I come back to the Midwest. I don't know how they can compete with one another; there seem to be so many. From the pedestrian's perspective, however, it is an unintended source of neighborhood beautification. We made our difficult choice from mounds of roses, carnations, and many other multicolored bouquets.

Back at the apartment we hunted for a suitable vase, and then gathered our things. The cab ride to the airport was surprisingly peaceful, and this driver took us the quickest route, and over our beloved Brooklyn Bridge, contributing to his tip. We arrived at the airport plenty early, especially since our plane was half an hour late boarding. That is just about the time that Murphy realized how lax he had been in executing his law within this vacation.

Once on board the plane, we took our seats and promptly began to sweat... a lot. I was a little too young for hot flashes, and Senator was definitely too male, so I ruled out menopause. The plane was filling up and everyone seemed overheated. *Oh, well, it should cool off when we get moving.*

I leaned over to the window to get comfortable. "Ouch!" The shade, though closed, was actually too hot to touch. This was definitely not right. We sat and sweated some more.

After half an hour or so, we were informed that the air conditioning unit was being fixed, and we would be leaving shortly. Lies, all lies. Two hundred irritated passengers sweated in unison, wondering why we couldn't at least get a drink of water. Our smelly cabin was not exactly living the glamorous jet-set lifestyle, and the first-classers were suffering right along with us. *So that's what you get for a $92 round-trip flight.*

An hour and a half late, we finally departed. The air was flowing now, circulating the odors efficiently. The drama continued when we landed. We collected our suitcase and eagerly went outside to catch the shuttle back to the parking lot. I looked up at the digital message board on the bus: Yellow Lot. Colors?! I don't remember anything about colored lots. We had taken whatever bus came by when we parked the car. I vaguely remembered that there were other lots, but last time we used the system, each bus made the rounds. Now the green lot bus pulled up, followed by the red.

We shrugged our shoulders and boarded yellow. It soon became apparent that it was the wrong bus. *This is why I don't gamble much when we go to Vegas.* I was pretty sure it was not green, so we transferred to red, wasting a good twenty minutes. Where was my poor Trucky? Eventually, at the final stop on the red route, I spotted my vehicle. We climbed off, tired and annoyed, but happy to get into some familiar wheels. It was an enjoyable weekend, but I was glad not to be flying anytime soon. Instead, I was already dreaming about a future road trip. *Murphy, schmurphy.*

Afterword

I sometimes stop and wonder if we should be spending so much time and money on travel, (although we do try to keep it within reason). Then I sit back and start to add up the price of all the cigarettes we don't smoke, all the beer and pop we don't drink, all the movies we don't see in the theatre, and the luxury cars that we definitely don't drive. When I am finished working my math magic, I come to the conclusion that we are actually behind a few trips. Thus, the addiction shows no sign of ebbing. Thank you for coming along for the ride. May you enjoy your own.

~Wendy V
June 2007

Appendix:
States Too Boring to
Safely Drive Through Alone

(listed in alphabetical order to prevent
further anger than this will already incite)

Arkansas
Illinois
Indiana
Iowa
Kansas
Nebraska
North Dakota
Oklahoma
Texas
Wyoming

(It should also be noted that various other states have specifically boring *parts* that should also be approached with great caution when driving alone.)

www.ingramcontent.com/pod-product-compliance
Lightning Source LLC
LaVergne TN
LVHW041629070426
835507LV00008B/531